IMAGINATION AND BEYOND: CRAFTING TIMELESS SUCCESS

A Case Study by Ridhima Kapur

Disclaimer

Acknowledgements

1. History of the company (cartoon formation)
2. SWOT AND PESTEL analysis
3. Organisational structure - table
4. Disneyland (expansion, first formed)
5. Evolution of Disney - OTT and black and white
6. Hospitality
7. Rights of Marvels and Starwars
8. Food and Beverage
9. Reference List

Disclaimer

This case study on The Walt Disney Company has been undertaken solely for educational purposes as part of academic research. The analysis, opinions, and interpretations presented in this work are those of the author, Ridhima Kapur, and do not reflect the views of The Walt Disney Company or any of its affiliates.

I have no association, formal or informal, with The Walt Disney Company, nor have I received any input, endorsement, or authorization from the company in the preparation of this study. All information used has been gathered from publicly available sources, and every effort has been made to ensure accuracy. However, this document should not be considered an official representation of Disney's business operations, strategies, or policies.

This study is intended for academic use only and should not be used for commercial or legal purposes.

Acknowledgements

I would like to express my heartfelt gratitude to those who supported me throughout the completion of this case study on The Walt Disney Company.

A special thank you to my parents for their unwavering encouragement and belief in me. Their support has been invaluable in this journey. I am also deeply grateful to my counselors—Arti Ma'am, Pavini Ma'am, and Yashi Ma'am—for their invaluable guidance and for providing me with this opportunity to undertake this research. Their insights and encouragement have been instrumental in shaping this work.

Lastly, a warm thank you to my cat, Bella, for her constant emotional support and for patiently listening to my drafts. Her comforting presence made the process all the more enjoyable.

This study has been a deeply enriching experience, and I am truly appreciative of everyone who contributed to it in their own special way.

History of Disney

We have all watched some or the other cartoon of Disney, whether it be Winnie the Pooh or Donald Duck. It is and always was a big part of our childhood "Walt Disney made his Alice Comedies for four years, but in 1927, he decided to move instead to an all-cartoon series. He created a character named Oswald the Lucky Rabbit to star in this new series. Within a year, Walt made 26 of these Oswald cartoons, but when he tried to get some additional money from his distributor for a second year of the cartoons, he found out that the distributor had gone behind his back and signed up almost all of his animators, hoping to make the Oswald cartoons in his studio for less money without Walt Disney. On rereading his contract, Walt realized that he did not own the rights to Oswald—the distributor did. It was a painful lesson for the young cartoon producer to learn. From then on, he saw to it that he owned everything that he made.The original Disney Studio had been in the back half of a real estate office on Kingswell Avenue in Hollywood, but soon Walt had enough money to move next door and rent a whole store for his studio. That small studio was sufficient for a couple of years, but the company eventually outgrew it, and Walt had to look elsewhere. He found an ideal piece of property on Hyperion Avenue in Hollywood, built a studio, and in 1926, moved his staff to the new facility. It was at the Hyperion Studio, after the loss of Oswald, that Walt had to come up with a new character, and that character was Mickey Mouse. With his chief animator, Ub Iwerks, Walt designed the famous mouse and gave him a personality that endeared him to all. Ub animated two Mickey Mouse cartoons, but Walt was unable to sell them because they were silent films, and sound was revolutionizing the movie industry. So, they made a third Mickey Mouse cartoon, this time with fully synchronized sound, and Steamboat Willie opened to rave reviews at the Colony Theater in New York November 18, 1928. A cartoon star, Mickey Mouse, was born. The new character was immediately popular, and a lengthy series of Mickey Mouse cartoons followed." ("Disney History") Walt Disney is an important part of the childhood of kids across the world. From Disney princesses to Mickey Mouse, all were possible because of the company Disney.

"Not one to rest on his laurels, Walt Disney soon produced another series—the Silly Symphonies—to go with the Mickey series. It featured different casts of characters in each film and enabled animators to experiment with stories that relied less on the gags and quick humor of the Mickey cartoons and more on mood, emotion, and musical themes. Eventually the Silly Symphonies turned into the training ground for all Disney artists as they prepared for the advent of animated feature films. Flowers and Trees, a Silly Symphony and the first full-color cartoon, won the Academy Award® for Best Cartoon for 1932, the first year that the Academy offered such a category. For the rest of that decade, a Disney cartoon won the Oscar® every year." Amazing movies have been made since then. "Disney has been a childhood cartoon for all of us. "The year 2011 saw the launch of the *Disney Dream* and the repositioning of the *Disney Wonder* to the West Coast. The Company purchased the rights to the *Avatar* franchise for theme parks, Aulani, A Disney Resort & Spa opened in Hawai'i, *The Little Mermaid: Ariel's Undersea Adventure* debuted at Disney California Adventure, and groundbreaking ceremonies were held for Shanghai Disneyland.

In theaters, Disney began distributing DreamWorks films, with *The Help* winning wide acclaim and a Supporting Actress Oscar for Octavia Spencer. Disney films included *Pirates of the Caribbean: On Stranger Tides, Winnie the Pooh, The Muppets* (Oscar for Best Song), and *Cars 2.*" ("Disney History") Disney's movies are said to be very fun and enjoyable for all ages. "In New York, *Sister Act* opened on Broadway and *Peter and the Starcatcher* off-Broadway. In theaters in 2012 were *John Carter, Brave, Wreck-It Ralph, Frankenweenie, Lincoln* (DreamWorks), and Marvel Studios' *The Avengers*. Bob Iger took on the additional title of chairman of the board, and Alan Horn became chairman of The Walt Disney Studios. The Disney Junior cable channel replaced SOAPnet. On Broadway, *Newsies* opened and won two Tony Awards. Cars Land opened at Disney California Adventure, and the *Disney Fantasy* set sail. At the Walt Disney World, Disney's Art of Animation Resort, an enlarged and enhanced Fantasyland, and a new *Test Track* opened. D23 sponsored a *Treasures of the Walt Disney Archives* exhibit at the Ronald Reagan Presidential Library and Museum. The big corporate news was the acquisition of Lucasfilm Ltd.

The beginning of 2013 saw a big achievement for Tokyo Disneyland. On April 15, it celebrated its 30th anniversary, naming it "The Happiness Year." New additions came to the theme parks, with Fantasy Faire opening in Disneyland and Mystic Point at Hong Kong Disneyland. Box office smashes, including *Iron Man 3* and *Thor: The Dark World* arrived in theaters. After 12 years, fans were able to travel back in time to see Mike and Sully go to school in *Monsters University,* and hearts melted in November when audiences adventured into the world of Arendelle for the first time with the Academy Award-winning film *Frozen*. The year 2014 got off to a great start with *Seven Dwarfs Mine Train* opening in Magic Kingdom at Walt Disney World. And, over at Walt Disney Studios Park at Disneyland Paris, *Ratatouille: L'Aventure Totalement Toquée de Rémy* made its debut. It was also a good year for films when the Company introduced audiences to a new, yet familiar set of horns when *Maleficent* premiered. *Guardians of the Galaxy* and *Big Hero 6* flew into theaters and were critical and box-office smashes.In 2015, the live-action film *Cinderella* reminded us to have courage and be kind. While the film provided many emotional moments, it wasn't long after that we came face-to-face with all of them—literally—with Disney•Pixar's *Inside Out*. Marvel Studios' *Ant-Man* debuted in July, and the fourth D23 Expo took place in August at Anaheim.

Then, that galaxy far, far away moved closer when *Star Wars: The Force Awakens* debuted in December.In 2016 *Zootopia* premiered in March. Then, animals of a very different kind pounced onto the screen in the live-action *The Jungle Book*. *Star Wars:* Galaxy's Edge had its official groundbreaking, and *Rogue One: A Star Wars Story* arrived in theaters on December 16. *Moana* and *Doctor Strange* were two other box-office smashes in 2016.Hong Kong became home to the first Marvel-themed ride at any Disney park in 2017 when *Iron Man Experience* opened. While guests were joining Iron Man in an epic adventure of a lifetime (as well as a fight against evil), guests at Walt Disney World traveled to a new world when Pandora—The World of Avatar opened in Disney's Animal Kingdom. May also saw the release of *Guardians of the Galaxy Vol. 2* and the opening of a new attraction, *Guardians of the Galaxy – Mission: BREAKOUT!* at Disney California Adventure." ("Disney History")

(Aithor)

"In 2003, Walt Disney came up with a movie called "Pirates of the Caribbean" which was a block buster hit at the box office. The movie was targeted for all the members of a family. In addition to the movie, Disney created a theme park ride, merchandising program, video game, TV series and comic books. In 2004, Disney presented the movie called "Home on the range" which was again a hit. Apart from the movie Disney created an accompanying soundtrack album, a line of toys for kids, clothing featuring the heroine, a theme park ride and a series of books. So Disney more often or not supports and promotes its movies with a host of secondary products attached to it. Disney's strategy is to build consumer markets for each of its characters, from classics like Mickey Mouse to snow white to new hits like Kim Possible. Each brand is created for a special age group and distribution channel. Disney has a large distribution channel. Baby Mickey Mouse and Disney babies target infants. Mickey Mouse is sold through the department and specially gift stores while Baby Mickey Mouse is a lower price option sold through mass-market channels.

Disney's Mickey's stuff for kids targets boys and girls while Mickey unlimited targets teens and adults." (Francis)

"The Walt Disney Company's main strength is in its resources, its experience in the business, and its low-cost strategy. Besides, the company has developed a very strong and well known "brand-name" through many years. The company has also been able to diversify its operations and products to hedge against decreasing sales in product lines. In recent years, it has categorized into Home Video, Film, merchandise, Radio broadcasting, Net-work television and in theme parks. It has also effectively diversified globally its operations from the USA to Japan and Europe." (Francis) Walt Disney is also said to have lots of strengths. "The Walt Disney Company's main strength is in its resources, its experience in the business, and its low-cost strategy. Besides, the company has developed clearly a very strong and well known "brand-name" through many years. The company has also been able to diversify its operations and products to hedge against decreasing sales in product lines. In recent years, it has categorized into Home Video, Film, merchandise, Radio broadcasting, Net-work television and in theme parks. It has also effectively diversified globally its operations from USA to Japan and Europe." (Francis) Disney has also had Television Channels like "Disney International HD" where shows like K.C Undercover, Girl Meets World, Austin and Alley were aired. A lot of teens have grown up watching these shows and still remember those good old days.

"The Walt Disney Company is facing several external opportunities. However, the external threats facing the company are out-numbering the opportunities. Opportunities include the following; positive government attitudes towards its operations, barriers of entry are significant, and include the entertainment industry itself. Legal and legislative forces are usually identified as negative external factors to the company. Furthermore, the French government contributed greatly to the Euro Disneyworld project in the Walt Disney Company's case. The French government invested in the project to build communication facilities, and gave the Walt Disney Company tax relief on the cost of

goods sold accounts. In addition, since the barriers of entry into the highly specialized industry in which the Walt Disney Company is still operating, competition will find it difficult to penetrate the company's highly diversified product or service mix. Therefore, large initial capital investments are required to enter the industry accordingly." (Francis)

"Walt had been developing Mickey for a while before he released the first animated shorts featuring Mickey, Plane Crazy and The Gallopin' Gaucho. Both of these films were silent and failed to find distribution; however, Disney's third sound-and-music-equipped short called Steamboat Willie, was a big hit, as Disney was the first to add a music and effect track to a cartoon. Walt still had more trends to set and boundaries to break. In 1929, Disney created Silly Symphonies, which featured Mickey's newly created friends: Minnie Mouse, Donald Duck, Goofy, and Pluto. One of the most popular cartoons, Flowers and Trees, was the first commercially released film produced in the full-color three-strip Technicolor process and it went on to earn Disney his second Academy Award, for Best Short." (Francis)

Disney has evolved from starting with silent films to films with dialogues. "Early in 2021, two Disney+ series from Marvel Studios became instant hits—*WandaVision*, which debuted in January, and *The Falcon and the Winter Soldier*, in March. Also in March, the animated *Raya and the Last Dragon* premiered to rave reviews on both Disney+ (with Premiere Access) and in theaters, and the new series *The Mighty Ducks: Game Changers* arrived on the streaming service, returning Coach Bombay (Emilio Estevez) to the ice. And, after more than a year of closure due to the pandemic, Disneyland Park welcomed guests back to Walt Disney's original magic kingdom on April 30, before Avengers Campus officially opened its gates at Disney California Adventure on June 4. The Walt Disney World Resort also prepared in earnest for its 50th anniversary festivities, kicking off The World's Most Magical Celebration on October 1, 2021. Featuring the opening of *Remy's Ratatouille Adventure* at EPCOT, and the debut of several new entertainment offerings, including Harmonious, also at EPCOT, and Disney Enchantment at Magic Kingdom Park, the 18th month celebration will welcome Guests from across the globe to help celebrate this momentous milestone." ("Disney History").

"The last film Walt produced at Laugh-O-gram was titled "Alice's Cartoonland." He recruited little four-year-old Virginia Davis, whom he had met while working for A.V. Cauger. Virginia had appeared in advertisements produced by Cauger's company and Walt thought she would be a good candidate to portray the title character in his new series of "Alice Comedies". Walt's concept for these cartoons was that they would involve a little girl who would, through a variety of circumstances, go to Cartoonland and would interact as a live-action character with animated animals and an animated environment. This concept was inspired by cartoons created by Max and Dave Fleischer's "Out of the Inkwell" series which had a cartoon character interacting with live-action characters and settings." (Dorsey).

"Shortly after completing that first Alice cartoon, Walt went into bankruptcy. He gave up on keeping his Kansas City studio operating after receiving no payment for the several cartoons he had produced under a contract he entered into with a church-based
company in Tennessee.Walt saved all the money he could put together to buy a first-class ticket to Los Angeles on the Atchison, Topeka & Santa Fe Railway. He left Kansas City in the late

summer of 1923, taking with him the one-reel Alice cartoon in a cardboard suitcase. However, before he left Kansas City, he made a point of taking his mouse companion out into the countryside so he would not fall victim to the cats which lived in the restaurant on the first floor of the Laugh-O-gram building.

Five years later, that mouse inspired the creation of the world's most famous fictional character, Mickey Mouse!" (Dorsey). "The Walt Disney Company launched its own television channel on April 18, 1983. The Original Disney Channel (1983-1997) marketed primarily towards younger children, with series such as Still the Beaver, The Baby-sitters Club, Five Mile Creek, Flash Forward, Adventures in Wonderland, Vault Disney, etc. In 1997, a new pre-teen programming took hold, with shows such as Smart Guy, Bug Juice, Jett Jacksons, and more. Later "Zoog Disney" attempted to connect the television and internet, giving kids who played online games an opportunity to see their names on television. From 2001 to 2002, Disney's ratings grew higher and it was about ninety percent basic cable programming. Pre-teens started watching the newer shows like, Even Stevens, Kim Possible, Lizzie McGuire and more, leading to the collapse of classic Disney programming. In recent years, the diversity of viewers has increased even more with an older audience of teenagers, young adults and families, from over one-hundred and sixty countries and twenty languages. Walt's interest in animating developed at a young age, as he drew and painted pictures to sell to his neighbors and family friends to earn extra money as a child. Walt quickly turned his hustle into a passion, as he enrolled in drawing and photography classes at McKinley high school and took classes at the Chicago Art Institute at night. Even when Walt was no longer in school, he continued to enhance his skills. He never stopped drawing, or trying to entertain others. No matter the trials and tribulations he faced, he never lost sight of his dream. When his first studio suffered from debt, he collaborated with his brother and old friend to open a new one. When his partners betrayed him and stole the rights to his first commercially successful character, Disney took it as an opportunity to release a new character. It is obvious Walt dedicated his life to his work, from his childhood to his death; thus, proving his love and dedication to animation is responsible for the success he has had in animating and the impact he continues to have on animation today." (Dorsey) The Disney Company's strength lies in its ability to tell stories that people of all generations resonate with, which is why the company endures to this day.

SWOT and PESTEL analysis

Any successful company has a lot of strengths and weaknesses.

Strengths are :

"Iconic Brand Recognition:

Disney's iconic brand recognition is undoubtedly one of the company's most significant strengths. The brand has been a household name for nearly a century, and it has become synonymous with entertainment and childhood memories for many generations. The company's brand is built on a foundation of beloved characters, timeless stories, and unforgettable experiences that have captured the hearts of millions of people around the world. Disney's brand recognition gives the company a significant competitive advantage and helps the company to create a solid emotional connection with consumers. In addition, Disney's brand recognition makes it easier for the company to expand into new markets and product categories. It also gives the company a robust platform for marketing and advertising.

I Diversified Portfolio:

Disney's diversified portfolio provides it with a range of products and services across multiple industries. The company's portfolio includes film and television production, theme parks, consumer products, and now, even streaming services. This diversity has enabled Disney to weather economic downturns and shifts in consumer preferences, making it one of the most stable and prosperous media conglomerates in the world.

The company's vast array of businesses ensures that if one industry experiences a downturn, other areas of the company can offset the losses."

(disney)

Weaknesses are :

"Dependence on specific franchises

While Disney boasts a vast portfolio of beloved franchises and characters, its heavy reliance on a few specific properties, such as Star Wars and Marvel, introduces inherent risks and challenges. Overdependence on other key brands can leave the company vulnerable to changes in consumer preferences and market trends. This is because the taste of the audience can shift, and what may be in high demand today might lose relevance or face saturation in the future. Also, an overdependence on specific franchises can lead to a lack of innovation and risk-taking. If a significant portion of Disney's resources, attention, and creative talent is dedicated to a few franchises, other potentially promising projects may receive less focus or investment.

High Operating Costs

The advantages of Disney's diversified portfolio are numerous; however, the substantial expenses associated with its operations create challenges that must be addressed. One of the primary factors contributing to Disney's high operating costs is the maintenance and operation of its theme parks and resorts worldwide. These iconic destinations, such as Disneyland and Walt Disney World, require extensive infrastructure, regular maintenance, and a large workforce to ensure optimal guest experiences. Also, the production and distribution of high-quality content is another reason for Disney's high operating costs. Whether it's producing blockbuster films, developing television shows, or creating animated features, Disney invests substantial financial resources in pre-production, production, marketing, and distribution. These costs include talent fees, production equipment, special effects, marketing campaigns, and the global distribution of films and television content. Finally, Disney is committed to technological innovation and advancement, hence the company's considerable investments in research and development to enhance its theme park experiences, develop cutting-edge visual effects for its films, and improve its digital platforms. These factors increase Disney's operation costs, taking a toll on the company's profitability and pricing strategies." (disney)

Opportunities are:

1. "Expansion into New Markets

As a global entertainment powerhouse, Disney has the potential to tap into untapped markets, reach new audiences, and diversify its revenue streams. Expanding into new markets will allow Disney to access a larger consumer base and increase its global presence. By entering new geographical regions, Disney would be opening doors to new revenue streams and growth opportunities. Also, expansion into new markets will help Disney to capitalize on emerging trends and cultural shifts. Finally, new markets present Disney with opportunities for strategic partnerships and collaborations. With this, the company can diversify its risk and reduce dependence on specific regions.

2. Increased Demand for Online Content

Disney's subscription video-on-demand and over-the-top streaming service, known as Disney+, is one of the company's famous product offerings. As the world increasingly embraces digital platforms and streaming services, Disney has the potential to capitalize on the growing appetite for online entertainment. The shift towards online consumption presents Disney with a vast and expanding audience base. The rise of streaming services and digital platforms allows Disney to have greater control over the distribution and monetization of its content. Through its streaming platform, Disney has direct access to its audience, and this approach provides Disney with more flexibility, allowing it to experiment with various pricing models, release strategies, and content formats." (disney)

Threats are :

1. Stiff Competition

Disney is a renowned entertainment company that operates in a highly competitive industry where rivals continuously vie for market share and consumer attention. The entertainment industry is characterized by intense competition from both traditional and emerging players. Major studios, streaming platforms, and content creators are constantly striving to capture audiences and deliver compelling content. The rise of digital platforms and social media has also given smaller content creators and influencers the ability to reach large audiences directly. Therefore, the competitive landscape increases the pressure on Disney to continually produce high-quality and innovative offerings that can stand out in a crowded market.

2. **Technological Disruptions**

Rapid technological advancements can disrupt traditional business models and consumer preferences in a dynamic landscape. Technological disruptions can alter how content is created, distributed, and consumed. Emerging technologies such as virtual reality (VR), augmented reality (AR), and artificial intelligence (AI) have the potential to disrupt the entertainment industry further. If Disney fails to adapt to these disruptions, it may result in a decline in audience reach and revenue generation. Technological advancements have also empowered content creators and independent studios to produce high-quality content at lower costs. Therefore, this might empower emerging creators and pose a threat to Disney's dominance, as they capture the attention of younger demographics and challenge the traditional model of content production and distribution." (disney)

These were a few strengths, weaknesses, opportunities, and threats of Disney. There is another way of analysis called the PESTEL analysis.

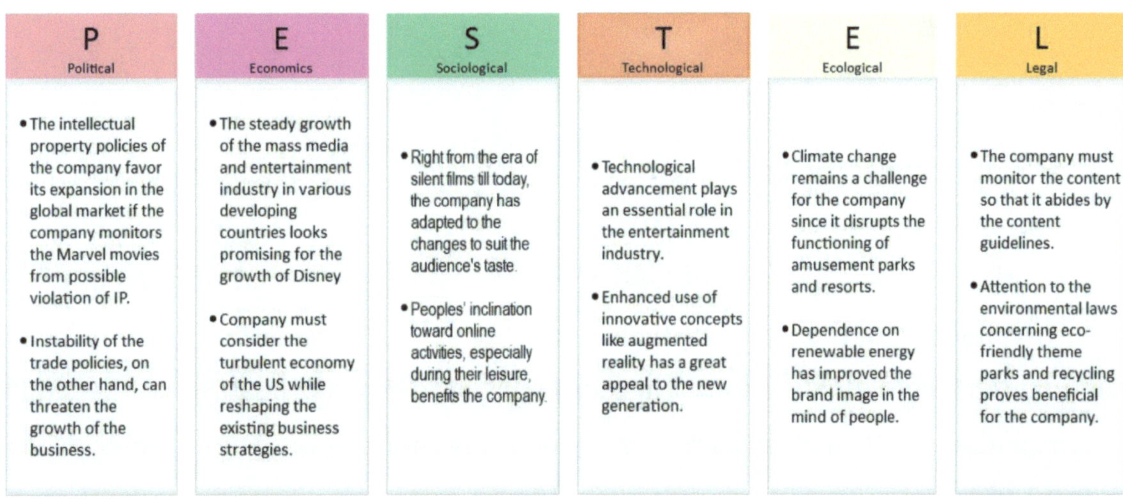

"**Political Factors:**

The political factors of a PESTEL analysis encompass the government laws, rules, and policies like internal political issues; leadership, foreign trade policy, corruption, political stability, taxation, and more, directly impact the finances of a company. It determines how the local or national government influences the business environment.

- As per the PESTEL analysis, the intellectual property policies of the company favor its expansion in the global market if the company monitors the Marvel movies from possible violation of IP.
- Instability of the trade policies, on the other hand, can threaten the growth of the business.
- The stable political condition of the major markets where the company operates provides the company with a competitive advantage over rivals.

Economic Factors:

Factors like unemployment, job growth, employment rate, interest and inflation rate, labor cost, purchase power of the consumers also influence the business environment. All these come under economic factors. It helps the company build its demand and supply model.

- The steady growth of the mass media and entertainment industry in various developing countries looks promising for the development of Disney, as indicated by Disney PESTEL analysis.
- However, the slow economic growth of countries that contribute a significant portion of the company's finances, like China, can threaten its progress.
- The company must consider the turbulent economy of the US while reshaping the existing business strategies.

Social Factors:

Social factors have an impact on the short-term and long-term goals of a business. These include cultures, traditions, norms, values, population, demographics, lifestyle, health and safety concerns, and other things. These manipulate the consumer attitude and buying pattern. Thus, affecting the profitability of the company.

- Right from the era of silent films till today, the company has adapted to the changes to suit the audience's taste. With time their content has matured and has become much more relevant.
- example - moana coco, encanto, culture vs cultural appropriation

- Peoples' inclination toward online activities, especially during their leisure, benefits the company.
- As per PESTEL analysis, the company's willingness to respect cultural diversity and create content keeping the taste and preference of the diverse audience in mind may help it achieve its long-term goal.

Technological Factors:

Technological innovation, automation, technical awareness, and more may affect the business positively or negatively. These factors come under technological factors. This factor affects production or manufacturing as well as the distribution of goods.

- Technological advancement plays an essential role in the entertainment industry. The use of advanced machines to create better content ensures growth opportunities for Disney, according to this Disney PESTEL analysis.
- Enhanced use of innovative concepts like augmented reality has a great appeal to the new generation. It works for the company's popularity.
- Increased mobile uses, the introduction of high-quality content, and interactive video games have worked in the company's favor.

Environmental Factors:

The emerging ecological issues have given rise to environmental awareness and sensitivity among companies. The scarcity of raw material, pollution, and such things must be considered while planning business strategies for a sustainable future.

- Climate change remains a challenge for the company since it disrupts the functioning of amusement parks and resorts.
- Dependence on renewable energy has improved the brand image in the mind of people.
- PESTEL analysis indicates that the company's initiatives related to environmental awareness, improved waste management system, eco-friendly theme parks, energy efficiency ensure growth opportunities.

Legal Factors:

If a business operates on a global market, legal metrics become more relevant. Equal opportunities, consumer rights, health & safety discrimination law, copyright laws, and others come under the legal parameters of PESTEL analysis.

- The company must monitor the content so that it abides by the content guidelines.

- Attention to the environmental laws concerning eco-friendly theme parks and recycling proves beneficial for the company.
- PESTEL indicates that improved strategies to protect consumer rights and copyright laws will help to thrive" ("Detailed PESTEL Analysis of Disney").

In conclusion, of the analysis this gives us a gist view about Disney.

<u>Organizational structure</u>

Disney is sadly not all about princes and princesses and fairy godmothers! A lot of highly qualified people day and night convert imagination into real life. One wonders about the difference between Disneyland and Disneyworld. "Among the biggest differences between Disneyland and Disney World is the resort size. It is 500 acres in size compared to Disney World's over 30,000 acres.Disneyland comprises two theme parks and three hotels, while the Walt Disney World Resort complex includes four theme parks, two water parks, 31 hotels and a golf course.The Walt Disney World and Disneyland resorts have their own hotels on property. However, Disneyland's options are much more scarce than Walt Disney World's. Within Disneyland, you'll find just three options from which to choose, with price points that vary based on luxury. At Walt Disney World, there are a whopping 31 on-site hotels. All of these feature incredible theming — such as overwater villas — and also run the gamut for pricing depending on where you stay." (Rawson and French) Who knew there was such a vast size difference between the two.

"The difference between the Disneyland castle versus the Disney World castle size is stark. The Disneyland castle, also known as the Sleeping Beauty Castle, is 77 feet tall. Disney World's Cinderella Castle, meanwhile, is more than double in size, standing 189 feet tall. While both castles are visually stunning, Disney World boasts a significantly grander and more imposing structure.Disneyland and Walt Disney World tickets start at a similar price range: Disneyland's tickets start at $104 for a one-day ticket, while Walt Disney World's tickets begin at $109 per day.However, Walt Disney World tickets will vary in price according to demand no matter what type of ticket you're purchasing; this is true for single-day and multiday tickets. For example, a four-day ticket for a visit in late August will cost $485. At Disneyland, multiday tickets are a fixed price. You'll be able to visit anytime and pay the same cost, no matter how busy it is. A four-day ticket to visit Disneyland costs $395." (Rawson and French)

We all have lived our childhood watching the Disney channel, from K.C undercover to Austin and Alley and what not. "In April 1983, The Disney Channel was established to bring high-quality, Disney-branded entertainment to the small screen. Forty years—and hundreds of iconic series and movies—later, the now-named Disney Channel offers a broad lineup of content ranging from live-action series and films to animated shows and shorts, which are unequivocal hits among kids and adults alike.

"For four decades, Disney Channel has been home to some of the most iconic and beloved stories in the Disney portfolio," says Ayo Davis, President, Disney Branded Television. "We are thrilled to celebrate this momentous anniversary with our incredible talent past and present, our gifted creative partners, and most importantly, with you—our passionate and loyal fans around the world. "Disney Channel has debuted award-winning series and movies that spawned passionate fandom, drove fashion trends, and helped drive the ascension of multi-hyphenate talent. From Tiger Town, High School Musical, Hannah Montana, Lizzie McGuire, That's So Raven, Wizards of Waverly Place, Jessie, and Descendants, to Phineas and Ferb, Kim Possible, Gravity Falls, and The Proud Family, Disney Channel has not only created meaningful memories for millions of kids and families, but also helped kickstart the careers of many beloved actors and artists and sent countless songs to the top of the charts. "When Disney Channel launched, it brought the magic of Disney storytelling into people's homes for the first time on a daily basis, and over the years it served as the most easily accessible and constant cultural touchpoint into the Disney brand," says Debra O'Connell, President, Networks & Television Business Operations, Disney Entertainment.

"Before they ever went to a Disney movie or hugged a beloved character at the Parks, many generations of people met their heroes for the first time on Disney Channel. That is a relationship that we cherish across the company today and is still unparalleled across the industry."As Disney Channel turns 40, it continues to build on this legacy with imaginative, award-winning programming that is beloved by both the young and young at heart— including current series Raven's Home, Big City Greens, Kiff, Hamster & Gretel, BUNK'D, Secrets of Sulphur Springs, The Villains of Valley View, Marvel's Moon Girl and Devil Dinosaur, and Saturdays, as well as the upcoming revival of Phineas and Ferb, new installments in the ZOMBIES franchise, and much more.

Fans can celebrate Disney Channel's 40th anniversary by watching an animated tribute video from Chibi Tiny Tales featuring fan-favorite characters from throughout the network's history, and by checking out fun throwback posts across Disney Channel's Instagram, Twitter, TikTok, and Facebook accounts, which will be shared all month long. Fans can also watch Disney Channel's YouTube channel, where full Disney Channel episodes, both old and new, are being live-streamed through the end of April." ("Disney Channel Celebrates 40 Years of Imaginative, Iconic Programming")

This talks about the isney channel and the evolution of it. There has to be some magic behind it right?

"Disney's mastery of its organizational structure is akin to a conductor leading an orchestra. Each segment and division plays its part in harmony, guided by strategic oversight and a visionary approach. This synergy is evident in how characters from its movies transition into theme park attractions or merchandise, creating a seamless, immersive experience for audiences worldwide. Moreover, Disney's approach to geographic localization ensures that its magic is universally accessible yet tailored to meet regional tastes and preferences. This local-global balance is a critical component of Disney's organizational strategy, enabling it to capture hearts across different cultures and demographics. Imagine stepping into a world where dreams materialize and stories unfold around every corner—a world meticulously sculpted by an orchestra of creativity, strategy, and precise organizational design. This world is none other than The Walt Disney Company's universe, a realm where the seamless integration of various business segments creates an unmatched entertainment experience. But what underpins this global powerhouse's ability to consistently captivate audiences across generations? The secret lies in its intricately woven organizational structure."

"Founded in 1923 by brothers Walt and Roy Disney, The Walt Disney Company has evolved into a leading American entertainment and media conglomerate renowned for its multi-faceted approach to business. At the heart of Disney's success is its multidivisional (M-form) organizational structure, a model that facilitates both specialization and cohesive brand synergy. This blog will embark on a journey to dissect Disney's organizational fabric, elucidate its components, and explore how it stands in comparison with other titans in the entertainment industry.By traversing through Disney's organizational landscape, readers will gain insights into how the company's strategic design fosters innovation, operational efficiency, and global market penetration. Let's unravel the magic behind Disney's organizational mastery and understand what makes it a beacon of success in the ever-evolving world of entertainment." (disney)

Cruises are pretty fancy, there are Disney cruises as well!

"The strength of Disney's brand makes it a bellwether of the cruise industry but it wasn't even a player just 25 years ago. The Mouse first dipped its toe in the water in the mid-1980s when it signed a partnership which allowed Premier Cruise Lines to sell combined cruise, hotel and theme park packages and offer on-board appearances from Disney characters. In 1993 Premier decided to partner with Warner Bros. instead and although it continued to offer land and sea packages with Disney's parks, it also added Universal Studios as an option. This led Disney to approach Carnival and Royal Caribbean about becoming its exclusive sea partner but the talks sank without a trace. In 1998 Disney decided to take the plunge and launched its own ship, the Disney Magic. The 85,000-ton liner has 875 rooms and an Art Deco style which evokes the golden age of cruising. The experience on-board is much more modern with appearances by cuddly characters and theaters showing Disney musicals. Disney founded the Magical Cruise Company to operate its fleet and chose to base the business in the UK which had a significant consequence. Disney's filings in the United States don't disclose the results of each of the individual businesses it owns but UK companies have to file documents which go into detail about their financial performance." (Forbes) Very interesting facts about cruises.

"As of 31st January 2023, "The company's fleet ship occupancy for financial year 2021 was 44% when operating. During 2021, ship occupancy levels were significantly lower than normal," says Magical Cruise Company director Tracy Wilson. "The company experienced increased cancellation and booking postponement requests which led to refunds, cruise credits of 125% of the reservation amount as well as future booking payment deferrals."

As a result of this, the cruise line's revenue dived by 86.5% to $98.7 million over the 12 months to 2 October 2021 according to its latest financial statements. However, its costs only fell by 27.3% to $732.6 million leaving it with a net loss which more than doubled to an all-time high of $629.5 million in 2021. The tide has turned since then.
"We have seen an increase in occupancy levels in FY22 to 55% as of June 2022," says Wilson. Reflecting this, the financial statements reveal that cruise deposits rose 28.6% to $537.8 million in 2021 and that trend is continuing.

"In financial year 2023, occupancy is anticipated to continually increase and exceed the comparable actual financial year 2022 quarterly levels," says Wilson. She adds that Disney expects the cruise line to "return to profitability in financial year 2023 as the industry recovers from a prolonged impact of COVID 19 and the business benefits from expanded capacity with the introduction of the Disney Wish, the company's fifth cruise ship."

The Disney Wish launched in June last year and was Disney's first new ship in a decade. It features the latest generation of Disney's water slide which has screens set into the side of the tubes to tell a story about Mickey Mouse whilst riders rocket past on rafts propelled by powerful jets of water. Built at Germany's Meyer Werft shipyard, the Disney Wish has 1,254 rooms and is valued in the financial statements at $1.4 billion, five times the amount that the Disney Magic is worth.

Disney will launch three more cruise ships over the next three years including one which will be the world's largest by passenger capacity as it will accommodate 6,000 people. Disney acquired it in November for a reported $44 million after its previous owner, Genting Cruise Lines, fell into administration. The ship is still under construction and the accounts reveal that the cost of completing it is "anticipated to be less than our recent fleet additions".

According to the financial statements, in 2021 the cruise line's headcount fell by 30.5% to 2,970, its lowest level in more than a decade, though staff pay only dropped 20.3% to $153.7 million. Staff numbers are set to swell with the launch of the new ships and the opening in 2024 of Disney's second private island in the Bahamas.
Despite this growth, Disney's cruise line will still be a minnow of the industry. Data from industry monitor CruiseMarketWatch shows that in 2021 Disney had just 2.2% of the market for passengers and 2.7% of the total revenue. It is a far cry from industry leader Carnival, which has a 37.1% share of revenue and carries a whopping 42% of the passengers."" (Forbes)

Disney Hotstar has reached a good audience, in India and all across the world.

"In urban India, OTT reach has grown from 28% in 2020 to 40% in 2021. India's current OTT audience stands at 621 million, as stated by Kantar in its 2022 ICUBE report. 30.7% of the OTT audience, amounting to 130.2 million people, fall under the SVOD (subscription video on demand) category. These subscribers have access to paid content, offering marketers the opportunity to target premium customers with seamless, engaging, and contextual ad formats. The remaining OTT audience (69.3%) that is accessing free content, is also the fastest growing category, widening the top of the funnel. Here, too, marketers can leverage effective CRM data and ad products to enhance full-funnel. Disney+ Hotstar: Expand reach across premium and regional audiences Disney+ Hotstar has emerged as the undisputed leader in the OTT segment with 80% of its reach coming from the 1 million plus towns. Regional content consumption contributes to over 40% of the platform's watch time. 72% of Disney+ Hotstar's subscribers reside at NCCS AB signifying a premium audience and therefore, greater potential for brand engagement." (Disney)

"Disney+ Hotstar stands out as the leading platform in terms of viewing experience and brand impact, surpassing the largest UGC OLV platform regardless of the ad type. Users on UGC OLV platforms are more inclined towards audio engagement rather than video. Consequently, when the same ad is played on an UGC OLV platform, the subsequent brand impact is notably lower compared to Disney+ Hotstar. Marketers should prioritise campaign effectiveness over mass reach when making choices. It is crucial to consider platforms like Disney+ Hotstar to ensure higher campaign effectiveness and maximise the impact on the target audience. By focusing on these insights, marketers can make informed decisions to optimize their advertising campaigns and achieve better results." (Disney)

We all have watched national geographic and been amazed by it. Whether it be different animals or different forests we see. NatGeo is also from disney. "Award-winning and critically acclaimed National Geographic Content, part of a joint venture between The Walt Disney Company and the National Geographic Society, creates and delivers riveting stories and experiences in natural history, science, adventure and exploration. Inspiring a deeper connection to the world, the content studio reaches 300 million people worldwide in 180 countries and 33 languages across the global National Geographic channels (National Geographic Channel, Nat Geo WILD, Nat Geo MUNDO), National Geographic Documentary Films, and direct-to-consumer platforms Disney+ and Hulu. Its diverse content includes Emmy® Award-winning franchise Genius, series Life Below Zero and Secrets of the Whales, and Oscar®- and BAFTA award-winning film Free Solo. In 2022, National Geographic Content was awarded eight News and Documentary Emmys, in addition to Life Below Zero's Emmy win for Outstanding Cinematography for a Reality Program, its sixth Emmy overall. For more information, visit natgeotv.com or nationalgeographic.com, or follow Nat Geo on Facebook, X, Instagram, YouTube and LinkedIn." (business wire)

In conclusion, this analysis gives us a view about the organizational structure about Disney.

Disneyland- The Beginning

"Walt Disney made his Alice Comedies for four years, but in 1927, he decided to move instead to an all-cartoon series. To star in this new series, he created a character named Oswald the Lucky Rabbit. Within a year, Walt made 26 of these Oswald cartoons, but when he tried to get some additional money from his distributor for a second year of the cartoons, he found out that the distributor had gone behind his back and signed up almost all of his animators, hoping to make the Oswald cartoons in his own studio for less money without Walt Disney. On rereading his contract, Walt realized that he did not own the rights to Oswald—the distributor did. It was a painful lesson for the young cartoon producer to learn. From then on, he saw to it that he owned everything that he made.

The original Disney Studio had been in the back half of a real estate office on Kingswell Avenue in Hollywood, but soon Walt had enough money to move next door and rent a whole store for his studio. That small studio was sufficient for a couple of years, but the company eventually outgrew it, and Walt had to look elsewhere. He found an ideal piece of property on Hyperion Avenue in Hollywood, built a studio, and in 1926, moved his staff to the new facility. It was at the Hyperion Studio, after the loss of Oswald, that Walt had to come up with a new character, and that character was Mickey Mouse. With his chief animator, Ub Iwerks, Walt designed the famous mouse and gave him a personality that endeared him to all. Ub animated two Mickey Mouse cartoons, but Walt was unable to sell them because they were silent films, and sound was revolutionizing the movie industry.

So, they made a third Mickey Mouse cartoon, this time with fully synchronized sound, and Steamboat Willie opened to rave reviews at the Colony Theater in New York November 18, 1928. A cartoon star, Mickey Mouse, was born. The new character was immediately popular, and a lengthy series of Mickey Mouse cartoons followed. Not one to rest on his laurels, Walt Disney soon produced another series—the Silly Symphonies—to go with the Mickey series. It featured different casts of characters in each film and enabled animators to experiment with stories that relied less on the gags and quick humor of the Mickey cartoons and more on mood, emotion, and musical themes. Eventually the Silly Symphonies turned into the training ground for all Disney artists as they prepared for the advent of animated feature films. Flowers and Trees, a Silly Symphony and the first full-color cartoon, won the Academy Award® for Best Cartoon for 1932, the first year that the Academy offered such a category. For the rest of that decade, a Disney cartoon won the Oscar® every year. While the cartoons were gaining popularity in movie houses, the Disney staff found that merchandising the characters was an additional source of revenue.

A man in New York offered Walt $300 for the license to put Mickey Mouse on some pencil tablets he was manufacturing. Walt Disney needed the $300, so he said okay. That was the start of Disney merchandising. Soon there were Mickey Mouse dolls, dishes, toothbrushes, radios, figurines—almost everything you could think of bore Mickey's likeness. The year 1930 was a big one for the mouse that started it all, as it saw the first Mickey Mouse book and newspaper comic strip published.

One night in 1934, Walt informed his animators that they were going to make an animated feature film, and then he told them the story of Snow White and the Seven Dwarfs. There were some skeptics in the group, but before long everyone had caught Walt's enthusiasm, and work began in earnest.

It took three years, but the landmark film debuted on December 21, 1937 and became a spectacular hit. Snow White soon became the highest-grossing film of all time, a record it held until it was surpassed by Gone with the Wind. Now Walt Disney's studio had firmer footing. The short cartoons paid the bills, but Walt knew that future profits would come from feature films. Work immediately began on other feature projects, but just as things were looking rosy, along came World War II. The next two features, Pinocchio and Fantasia, were released in 1940. They were technical masterpieces, but their costs were too high for a company losing most of its foreign markets because of the war. Dumbo was made in 1941 on a very limited budget, but Bambi, in 1942, was another expensive film, and caused the studio to retrench. It would be many years before animated features of the highest caliber could be put into production." ("Disney History") Disney has been around for a long time now, our parents also have grown up watching Disney. "In 1994, Disney ventured onto Broadway with a very successful stage production of *Beauty and the Beast*, followed in 1997 by a unique staging of a show based on *The Lion King* and in 2000 by *Aida*. By restoring the historic New Amsterdam Theatre on 42nd Street, Disney became the catalyst for a successful makeover of the famous Times Square area. A musical version of *The Hunchback of Notre Dame* opened in Berlin, Germany in 1999. By 1996, there were more than 450 Disney Stores worldwide, and by 1999 that number was up to 725.

In Florida, the first home sites were sold in the new city of Celebration, located next to Walt Disney World. Eventually, 20,000 people would call Celebration their home. After the death of the owner Gene Autry, Disney acquired the California Angels baseball team to add to its hockey team, and in 1997 opened Disney's Wide World of Sports at Walt Disney World. Early in 1996, Disney completed its acquisition of Capital Cities/ABC. The $19 billion transaction, second-largest in U.S. history, brought the country's top television network to Disney, in addition to 10 TV stations, 21 radio stations, seven daily newspapers, and ownership positions in four cable networks.The years that followed saw the release of a group of very popular live-action films, such as *Mr. Holland's Opus*, *The Rock*, *Ransom*, *Flubber*, *Con Air*, *Armageddon*, and culminating in the hugely successful *The Sixth Sense*, which soon reached the 10th spot among the all-time highest grossing releases. Computer animation was showcased in *a bug's life* and *Dinosaur*.

A whole new park, Disney's Animal Kingdom, opened at Walt Disney World in 1998. With a gigantic Tree of Life as its centerpiece, the park was Disney's largest, spanning 500 acres. A major attraction was the *Kilimanjaro Safaris*, where Guests could experience live African animals in an amazingly accurate reproduction of the African savannah. An Asian area opened at Animal Kingdom in 1999. Back in California, Tomorrowland at Disneyland was redesigned in 1998. As the world moved toward a new century, Epcot became the host of Millennium Celebration, *Test Track* (the longest and fastest Disney park attraction) opened, and other attractions were revised and updated. The Walt Disney Company welcomed a new president—Robert A. Iger—and the Company reached the $25 billion revenue threshold for the first time. Disney regional entertainment expanded with DisneyQuest and the ESPN Zone in 1998, and that same year, the *Disney Magic,* the first of two luxury cruise ships, made its maiden voyage to the Caribbean, stopping at Disney's own island paradise, Castaway Cay. The year 2000 opened with the release in IMAX theaters of an almost totally new version of *Fantasia* entitled *Fantasia/2000*. Other classically animated features were *The Emperor's New Groove, Atlantis: The Lost Empire, Lilo & Stitch, Treasure Planet,* and *Brother Bear*. Continuing collaborations with Pixar brought the computer-animated blockbuster *Monsters, Inc.* Popular live-action productions continued with *Remember the Titans, Mission to Mars, Pearl Harbor, The Princess Diaries*, and *The Rookie*. The new cable network, SoapNet, was launched, and award-winning productions on ABC included *The Miracle Worker, Anne Frank*, and *Child Star: The Shirley Temple Story*." ("Disney History")

"Before it became a company with an $187 billion market cap,1 with interests spanning the globe, Disney was more closely associated with the vision of the man after whom it was named. It was this vision that laid the groundwork for the company to become the media giant it is today. March 20, 2019, Disney officially acquired all the media assets of 21st Century Fox for $71.3 billion, making it the largest media powerhouse on the planet.Pixar, Marvel, and the Star Wars empire were already a part of Disney's stable of mega-brands, but the acquisition of 21st Century Fox brings the rest of Marvel Entertainment into the Mouse's house, including the X-Men, Fantastic Four, and Deadpool franchises. The deal also gave Disney former Fox television networks such as FX Networks and National Geographic, in addition to Fox's 30 percent ownership of the streaming platform Hulu, which gives Disney a controlling share of 60 percent. Disney launched its own streaming service, Disney+, in a blow to Netflix, which has licensed several key parts of the Disney library." ("walt disney")

Disney's first blockbuster was "Snow White and the Seven Dwarfs," that is something new! "In 1937 the release of Disney's first full length-animated film, "Snow White and the Seven Dwarfs," in Technicolor, goes on to become the most successful sound film of all time. Decades before Pixar, Dreamworks and others would perfect the animated art of giving all ages of moviegoers the sniffles at the theater, the animation and color of "Snow White" would bring a tear to the eye of one film critic. From the review in Daily Variety, Dec. 22, 1937: "Walt Disney's animation of Grimm's fable, 'Snow White and the Seven Dwarfs,' sets a milestone in the art of picture making. It is completely a thing of beauty and charm. … 'Snow White' is the genius of craftsmanship which can make an endless series of line drawings and color washes so eloquent in human expression and trouble and antic joy, so potent in evoking audience emotion, laughter, excitement, suspense, tears. Yes, indeed — tears!" " (Snow White becomes highest)

"Disney's evolution from a little cartoon studio into the largest entertainment company in the world has resulted in a far more complicated legacy in film than many realize. Of the 55 films to ever cross $1 billion at the global box office, Disney's library encompasses over half of them. They also own all 5 of the highest grossing movies ever released theatrically. Once one of the smallest dream factories in Hollywood, the company's film studio is now a behemoth. Below is an attempt to create as accurate a list as possible of their 500+ highest grossing movies out of the 5,000+ they've ever owned or released. I created this because I couldn't find something that wove together films from their more obvious studios (Walt Disney Pictures, Marvel, Pixar and Lucasfilm) along with brands often less directly associated with Disney (20th Century, Searchlight, Buena Vista International, Touchstone, Hollywood, Miramax and Dimension). So while this list is less focused solely on the company's storied core brand, it's also arguably a far more vivid reflection of the diverse universe of movies that have fallen within the walls of the mouse house over the years. I've also included a note below each title explaining how it ties back to the company and its estimated global theatrical box office." (everythingdiz)

Walt Disney was a hardworking man. "At just the age of seven, he sold his first drawings. Due to financial troubles, two years later, he started helping his father deliver newspapers. However, he continued honing his drawing skills and developing his art education.

At the age of 18, he had his first encounter with animation in Pesman Art Studio, where he met a fellow artist named Ub Iwerks. Disney and Iwerks soon had a failed attempt at creating their own commercial company, and later on, Disney founded another company, a film studio, where he employed Iwerks, among others, as an animator.

In 1923 Disney had to declare bankruptcy due to high costs, resulting in his second entrepreneurial attempt. Nevertheless, his work in the animation industry didn't go unnoticed, earning him a contract that led to the Disney Brothers Cartoon Studio's first production, a series named "Alice comedies" which mixed live-action motion-picture photography with cartoon animation. One of the first such productions.

Disney worked on the series until 1927, with his friend and former partner Iwerks producing more than 50 films. His next creation, "Oswalt the Lucky Rabbit", was produced for Universal Studios and was a hit. However, during negotiations, he realized that he had painted himself into a corner, signing away all of the rights for Oswalt when he accepted the contract and losing all of his animators, except for Iwerks, to Universal Studios.

Disney and Iwerks went on and created Mickey Mouse as an answer, retaining all the rights this time. Disney lent his voice to Mickey and Iwerks drew him. Together they created the first cartoon with synchronized sound, the short film "Steamboat Willie", which was the first film with Mickey that had a distributor and was the start of the mouse's exploding career. Actually, the film was so successful and significant as an innovation that in 1998 was added to the National Film Registry by the United States Library of Congress." (Disney) This talks a little about Walt Disney's life and his success.

"In the last decade, Disney has started capitalizing on nostalgia. It recognizes that their once upon a time young audience has now grown up, having its own kids and family. Parents remember the feelings of excitement and joy they experienced when they were watching Disney's animation films as young children and want their kids to have the same experience.

Over the last years, Disney understands this and has proved it, developing live-action movies of their old and popular animation films targeting the parents more than the children. The success of that tactic is evident in movies like "The Lion King" which grossed over $1.5 million in 2019.

Technology today offers an unprecedented opportunity to remake old classics into live-action adaptations with stunning visuals and incredibly realistic CGIs. And Disney still has a lot of content in its library to use and exploit the feeling of nostalgia." (disney)

Evolution of Disney - OTT and black and white

Disney wasn't always what it is today, it evolved from being black and white to coloured and the characters changed from time to time.

"As Disney has been enthusiastically reminding us all year, 2023 marks the 100th anniversary of the founding of the Disney Brothers Cartoon Studio by Walt and Roy Disney. Walt was an animator whose previous company, Laugh-o-Gram Studio, which he founded with Ub Iwerks, had just gone bankrupt. Meanwhile Roy was still suffering from tuberculosis. Yet the studio they founded would come to be ranked number 53 on the Fortune 500 list of the biggest companies in the United States in 2022. More impressive still, the company has achieved the ever elusive mystique of being a brand adored and respected around the world. The Walt Disney Company (as it has been known since 1986) has expanded into all sorts of areas over the years, from theme parks to superhero movies to streaming documentaries, but the heart and soul of the endeavour is still, at the end of things, Walt Disney Animation Studios, which was put into its own division in 1986. The studio's latest animated feature film, Wish, is its 62nd, and it continues Disney's century-old tradition of constantly innovating and evolving its art, sound, and storytelling." (Harrisson)

It takes a lot for one animated movie to be made. From voiceovers to character designing, to timing it perfectly.

"In traditional hand-drawn animation, character designers produce model sheets to finalize each character's appearance and how they move. In computer animation, 3D animators create virtual skeletons with a series of key movements using digital software. In computer animation, computer programs then handle movements between these core moves. In traditional animation, animators produce individual drawings for every moment of the film—24 frames per second, that is, 24 separate drawings for every second of screen time. These are then passed to the Ink and Paint department to be outlined in ink and, finally, painted with color. During the 1940s, this department was primarily staffed by young women. Disney animation has undergone a few shifts in style over the years. The most obvious was the shift to 3D CGI. Having used some computer generated imagery and techniques to speed things up (and make editing possible) in *The Black Cauldron*, Disney used computer animation for some backgrounds in *The Great Mouse Detective* (1986), and for a two-minute sequence inside a clock tower. Computer animation allowed the camera to pan around a three-dimensional space rather than back and forward across a flat surface. They put this to real effect in the ballroom scene 1991's *Beauty and the Beast*. The ballroom was the first entirely computer generated environment, with only the characters being hand-drawn. This was done so that the camera could swirl around them as they danced. This was followed with *Aladdin* in 1992, which featured one of the earliest computer generated speaking characters in a feature film, the Cave of Wonders, which was CGI as it was technically part of the background (the very first was a glass knight in *The Young Sherlock Holmes* in 1985). *Aladdin*'s Magic Carpet was also Disney's first hybrid of hand-drawn and computer animation, with CGI used to fill in its pattern." (Harrisson)

For example, Moana, which brought a new aspect into the disney movies is inclusive of all colours. Racial discrimination is a big topic today and all the princesses always seem to be perfect. Moana is different because she has a darker shade, which shows Disney is trying to be inclusive of all the skin colours. There are many more societal issues which Disney is being inclusive of.

"As popular trends come and go, Disney is almost forced to change so that it can continue to appeal to a broad range of people. Of course, those who don't agree with a trend or don't follow it can become angry or confused with Disney's decision-making. But if Disney doesn't keep up with the latest trends, or even stay ahead of them and set their own, it runs the risk of falling behind.It's clear that Disney recognizes this — and you have to admit that it stays pretty trendy. We witness this regularly with the trends in the parks — Instagrammable walls, rose gold merchandise, and even street parties, which have taken the place of most parades." (AllEars) Disney is still in trend because it keeps on changing with time, it keeps up with the latest trends and what each and every generation likes. For example Inside Out was released in 2015 and they waited, to post the second movie, for the generation watching it to grow up to understand the new emotions like Anxiety and Jealousy.

Disney movies are also available on OTT platforms and can be streamed anytime and anywhere. In India,there is an OTT platform called Disney+Hotstar and there are many many disney movies on the same.

"Disney has invested heavily in Hulu and expects to invest even more after it consolidates the asset as a result of the purchase of 21st Century Fox. Hulu and ESPN+ create an interesting pair that is likely to start merging into the Disney platform. Each offers distinctive sports programming, and the union will bring a richer sports offering. Moreover, Disney's streaming service is likely to develop into a global platform, bringing the company to operate globally in TMT supply modes as a platform that adds proprietary video programming on top of third-party distribution capacity. Because the number one global distributor of movies is seeking to vertically disintegrate and become a platform, this will likely create a context where more TV entertainment demands, which can be met via the Internet, are met directly by selling into global streaming platforms. The final section will discuss the changes brought about by this move that is driven by the changing structure of supply for premium TV programming. Disney's recent purchase of 21st Century Fox has created some fuss about whether it is going to aim to take Netflix head-on. At the completion of the purchase, Disney will effectively hold 60 percent of Hulu, the low-cost service that would be integrated with Disney's own platform in a TV-focused pair that would not be directly competitive with Netflix. As noted earlier, geopolitical concerns and the ability of European and other local TV content suppliers to bring their assets to Netflix are likely to limit Disney's global ambition. Nevertheless, it is possible for Disney to create a Hulu- or ESPN+ US-focused pair with its own platform that offers distinct TV sports functionalities, including in stages the next US Olympics, potentially drag racing, golf, ice skating, fishing, and other sports with small but dedicated fan communities that fear being shunted by dominant entities and are looking for a niche supplier that will maintain discipline on distribution prices." (Aithor)

There are perfect movies also to watch on disney+ Hotstar.

"**<u>Up</u>**

Prepare to be moved and inspired by this endearing Disney film that has touched the hearts of countless people and will undoubtedly do the same for you. Meet Carl, a widower committed to fulfilling his late wife's wish of traveling to Paradise Falls to build a house. Along the way, he encounters a young child named Russell, and together they overcome numerous challenges. Will Carl's adventure be successful? Grab some tissues and watch as this heartwarming narrative unfolds.

OTT platform: Disney Plus Hotstar

<u>Ratatouille</u>

This uplifting Disney classic places the idea that "anyone can cook" at its core. Follow Remy's incredible journey as he battles prejudice against rodents in society and pursues his passion for cooking. Through a chance encounter, he befriends Linguini, a young man who becomes an unexpected ally. Together, they defy expectations and prove that true talent knows no bounds. Prepare to be touched and captivated by this charming tale of friendship, dreams, and the importance of self-belief.

OTT platform: Disney Plus Hotstar

The BFG

Get ready to be comforted and enchanted by this touching Disney film! Follow Sophie's captivating adventure as she befriends a giant with a noble mission: to save people from menacing giants who threaten them. Witness the remarkable bond that develops between Sophie and her colossal companion as they embark on an epic journey that will tug at your heartstrings and serve as a reminder of the power of courage and friendship.

OTT platform: Sony Liv

Big Hero 6

Prepare to be swept away on an emotional rollercoaster in this captivating Disney film set in a futuristic society where robots not only serve food but also offer healing. Follow young protagonist Hiro as he seeks revenge against those who took his brother's life. Experience a thrilling and endearing adventure of bravery, camaraderie, and the pursuit of justice with the help of Baymax and a group of companions.

OTT platform: Disney Plus Hotstar

Raya and the Last Dragon

Embark on the captivating journey of Raya, a determined young girl whose father's goal is to reunite their divided world, known as Kumandra, in this recent Disney film. They place their trust in the legendary dragon "Sisu" to aid them in achieving this ambitious objective. Follow Raya on her daring mission to restore peace and discover whether their world can truly unite despite the challenges and obstacles they face.

OTT platform: Disney Plus Hotstar, Apple TV+

Zootopia

This Disney film exemplifies the saying "Anyone can be anything they want to be." Witness Judy's extraordinary journey as she strives to fulfill her dream of becoming a police officer. Despite facing opposition, she takes on an impossible task. Join her and Nick, a fox, in an unlikely partnership as they work together to solve a captivating case. Explore the power of determination, friendship, and the belief that no aspiration is too grand in this joyful and thrilling tale.

OTT platform: Disney Plus Hotstar, Apple TV+" (Goel)

It takes a lot to make one single animated film, Voiceovers and music etc. "Snow White and the Seven Dwarfs (1937), as well as being the first full length animated feature film, was also the first movie to have a commercially issued soundtrack released. Music has been a key ingredient to the success or failure of Disney animated films ever since, especially in the hugely successful period known as the Disney Renaissance, which lasted roughly between 1989 and 1999.

While songs had never disappeared entirely from Disney animation, they had become a much less integral part of the films during the 1970s and 1980s. For example, The Black Cauldron did not include any songs at all. All that changed when it was decided that The Little Mermaid (1989) should be a full musical, with numerous songs sung by the characters and forming an integral part of the story. The songwriting team from 1982's off-Broadway hit Little Shop of Horrors, composer Alan Menken and lyricist Howard Ashman, were hired and the rest, as they say, is history. Ashman tragically passed away from complications due to AIDS in 1991 after contributing to the Oscar-winning music of Mermaid, Beauty and the Beast, and Aladdin (and more or less defining what a modern Disney musical's storytelling structure should be), but Menken continued to work on numerous Disney films through the 1990s and some after, most recently animated classic Tangled in 2010 and Disenchanted in 2022.

Tim Rice had to finish Ashman's work on Aladdin, which had been Ashman's original pitch, but the music was not the only notable thing about that film. Comedy superstar Robin Williams was hired to voice the wacky, over-the-top character of the Genie on the agreement that neither his name nor image would be used for marketing—a condition that perhaps inevitably was not met.

Aladdin was not the first Disney film to include celebrity cast members. Robin Hood (1973) cast big name British actors Peter Ustinov and Terry Thomas as its villains, and Billy Joel and Bette

Midler both appeared in Oliver and Company (1988). But the impact of the Genie as well as the next two films, The Lion King (1994) and Pocahontas (1995), was huge. Pocahontas also featured a major star in Mel Gibson as John Smith, and The Lion King was filled with celebrity voices including James Earl Jones, Whoopi Goldberg, Matthew Broderick, and Nathan Lane, not to mention songs by Elton John. Thanks in no small part to the success of Aladdin and The Lion King, animated movies for the past couple of decades have been filled with star voices.

Those voices also include, like The Lion King, both actors and singers. After Enchanted made the baffling decision to cast Broadway star Idina Menzel and then not have her sing, Frozen (2013) famously put that right with the bane of every parents' existence, the mega-hit "Let It Go." Hits like that and the cachet of a Broadway star like Menzel have ensured that Disney's recent animated classics are, like The Little Mermaid and Beauty and the Beast before them, fully fledged musical films." (Harrisson) Disney movies show a few themes throughout the spam of the movie for example, black and white movies show racism. A few examples of these movies are :

- **"Lady and the Tramp (1955):** Two Siamese cats, Si and Am, are depicted with anti-Asian stereotypes. There is also a scene at a dog pound where heavily-accented dogs all portray the stereotypes of the countries their breeds are from - such as Pedro the Mexican Chihuahua, and Boris the Russian Borzoi
- **The Aristocats (1970):** A Siamese cat called Shun Gon, voiced by a white actor, is drawn as a racist caricature of an Asian person. He plays the piano with chopsticks
- **Dumbo (1941):** A group of crows that help Dumbo learn how to fly have exaggerated stereotypical black voices. The lead crow is called Jim Crow - a reference to a set of racist segregationist laws in the southern US at the time - and he is voiced by a white actor, Cliff Edwards
- **Jungle Book (1968):** The character of King Louie, an ape with poor linguistic skills, sings in a Dixieland jazz style and is shown as lazy. The character has been criticised for being a racist caricature of African-Americans
- **Peter Pan (1953):** The film refers to Native people as "redskins", a racist slur. Peter and the Lost Boys also dance in headdresses, which Disney now says is a "form of mockery and appropriation of Native peoples' culture and imagery". A song originally

called "What makes the red man red" was also decried as racist - it was later renamed as "What makes the brave man brave"

- **<u>Song of the South (1946):</u>** One of Disney's most controversial movies, which has never been released on video or DVD in the US. Its depiction of plantation worker Uncle Remus perpetuates an old racist myth that slaves were happy in the cotton fields" ("Disney updates content warning for racism in classic films")

"Disney has a long history of using racial caricatures in its films that reinforce negative stereotypes. In The Princess and the Frog, Princess Tiana, the only Black Disney princess, is not fully represented. For three-quarters of the film, Tiana is a frog, symbolizing Disney's reluctance to depict a Black princess. In fact, the only main African-American character in the movie who remains human is the villain.

Tiana is also the only Disney princess whose storyline revolves around her financial struggles. While Sleeping Beauty, Cinderella, Snow White, and Ariel all come from wealthy families and live in castles, Tiana works two jobs and her mother cleans houses. It is Tiana's dream to own a restaurant, however, she does not achieve this dream until the end of the movie when she marries a man and he assists her in purchasing a restaurant. This demonstrates the franchise's belief that a woman cannot achieve her dreams without the assistance of a man, as well as Disney's belief that Tiana must struggle with financial difficulties as a result of her race. When compared to other Disney princesses, Tiana is clearly characterized as the "Black servant," presenting Tiana and her mother within the same narrow scope of historical representations of Black womanhood.

Seven out of the 11 Disney princesses are white, according to mediamilwaukee.com. These ethnic princesses do not display the same feminine and beautiful attributes as white princesses. Snow White, Sleeping Beauty, and Belle all wear gowns, gloves, and have neatly-done hair. Disney also depicts these white princesses as well mannered and feminine. Princesses of color, however, do not share these elegant characteristics.   Mulan, an Asian princess, is a warrior, Pocahontas is depicted as "savage like," Moana is known for her rebellion, and Jasmine wears pants. This exemplifies Disney's depiction of white as beautiful and civilized and people of color as "other."

The hyenas from Disney's film, the Lion King, symbolize racist stereotypes of gang groups and depict anti-Hispanic undertones. Courtesy of disneyfandom.com

In Disney films, there is undeniable evidence of white privilege and binary color symbolism that associates white with goodness and black with evil. Snow White and the Seven Dwarfs features a wicked queen dressed in black, who lives in a black castle, has   black rats, and there is a dangerous black forest containing black bats and black owls. On the contrary, Snow White is surrounded by white birds, the Prince rides a white horse, Snow White is laid to rest on white flowers, and after the Prince rescues her they ride off together towards a white castle." (Hart)

Disney leaves movies at cliff hangers, making the audience more curious about what's going to happen next and that pushes Disney to make sequels for the same.
"Of the most successful movies of the last decade, I'd bet nine out of 10 were sequels. As someone who goes to the movie theater a lot, I feel like a majority of advertised films are sequels. They're everywhere. I think it's fair to say a lot of moviegoers are sick of franchises and constant cash-ins. I remember watching 2024's notoriously trashy "Madame Web" in a movie theater and hearing audible groans when the trailer for "Ghostbusters: Frozen Empire" played.

I didn't watch the fifth "Ghostbusters" film, and I'm not going to watch "Inside Out 2" or "Mufasa: The Lion King" — something I couldn't believe was real and releasing later this year — because I have zero interest and think they feel lazy.

But the truth is that no matter how much people roll their eyes at reboots, sequels, and prequels — they make money.

Disney is the most notorious for making unnecessary sequels. I'd argue it's been a part of its brand since the '90s when they released cheaply made direct-to-VHS and -DVD sequels to their theatrical hits.

After "The Lion King" was released in 1994, there was a TV series, TV movie, and two direct-to-video movies within the span of 10 years. Making sequels isn't new for Disney.

Besides, sequels are a necessity for the studio nowadays. People are less and less inclined to see movies at the theater, where studios make the most profit off of their productions, and instead wait for the film to appear on their TVs via numerous streaming services.

"Top Gun: Maverick," "Spider-Man: No Way Home," and "Avatar: The Way of Water" are the most profitable films in the post-pandemic era, all of which are sequels. With the convenience of staying home to watch movies and the increase in ticket prices at theaters nationwide, audiences have proven they will only show up for trusted, reliable brands.

Thus, we get "Inside Out 2," the most recent Disney sequel, which has garnered the largest opening weekend of any movie this year.

Disney's three big brands — Marvel, Star Wars, and Pixar — have lost a lot of steam in recent years with poor box office performances and a dilution of quality, thanks to an onslaught of streaming TV, which most people, myself included, forgot about or never got around to watching.

Pixar specifically has suffered the most since its last five films vastly underperformed, resulting in 14 percent of the company being laid off last month, the first time layoffs have hit the studio in its 30 years of moviemaking.

Sequels do good business — and Hollywood is a business.

In order to keep movie theaters populated and keep studios running, sometimes cash-ins are needed. As someone who loves theaters and spends way too much money on movie tickets, I would hate to see them go away. The movie business is in a dire state right now, and if Disney sequels keep it running, then I say bring me a Ratatouille Cinematic Universe." (Dunn and Hickman)

Hospitality of Disney

Disney also provides hospitality under various categories for example colleges, hotels, cruises, parks etc.

"Over 80 years ago Walt Disney institutionalized the Kansas City Film Ad Company, which would not only develop into a paramount film production corporation, but also would set the standards for hospitality and tourism as we know it. The Disney brothers launched this small animation studio in Missouri, producing a string of animated short and full length motion pictures. They were ambitious men, who maintained that resourcefulness and innovation would lead to their company's success. This theory is ever prevalent and lies behind the company's continued growth. The studio produced numerous films, receiving a considerable amount of notoriety throughout the United States, when the Disney brothers first began generating film related merchandise. What had seemed like an insignificant investment actually began the corporation's consumer product line and business division. Their production company was unsurpassed and merchandise sales were on the rise, but never settling, the brothers anxiously explored something fresh and innovative to maintain the growth of their studios. After several years of development, Disneyland California opened July 17, 1955, marking the beginning of their great impact on the hospitality and tourism world. Since its self-effacing development in 1923 the Walt Disney Company has continued their devotion to unrivaled entertainment and loyalty to their guests. The guest experience branches out into four distinct areas spanning consumer products and merchandise, media coverage (including ESPN and ABC), resorts and entertainment, and major production studios. Beginning with the Disneyland Resort in Anaheim California, the corporation's parks and resorts have grown controlling 11 theme parks including the celebrated Walt Disney World Resort in Lake Buena Vista Florida, Tokyo Disney, Disneyland Resort Paris, and Hong Kong Disneyland. In addition the company has broadened its horizons with world class cruise lines traveling the Caribbean and Mediterranean. Though there are numerous Disney resorts throughout the world the company maintains the highest level of commitment to all guests, and offer many benefits including complimentary resort transportation, internet access, private in room babysitting, wheelchair accessibility, and extra magic hours (extra park hours only available to resort guests). There are four major categories of resorts offered to guests, Disney Deluxe Villa Resorts, Disney Deluxe Resorts, Disney Moderate Resorts, and lastly Disney Value Resorts. Due to the corporation's faithfulness and loyalty to its millions of patrons from year to year it has experienced a virtually unremitting stretch of development since its early founding's. The company employs over 130,000, "cast members," and has returned over and above thirty billion dollars a year on average. Its impacts on our society are unsurpassed and affect the lives of every person every day." (Celinayebba)

Disney hotels are very fancy as seen in the picture, they have all animated related things like having mickey mouse pancakes and having all decorations of various movies and all the animated characters having some resemblance to the hotel.

"The Walt Disney World College Program is a national paid-internship program owned and operated by the Walt Disney Company, and it could be your ticket into a career at the Magic Kingdom. College-age students can apply to take part in a program that is highly competitive and quite rigorous. But it could also give you a distinct advantage in becoming a part of Disney's unique culture and diverse community. If you're a college student with an interest in joining one of the world's best-known and most beloved entertainment brands, and you don't mind answering to a giant mouse, the Disney College Program could be just what you're looking for.

And for a sense of what the Disney College Program is really like, we spoke with program graduate, Jennifer Tatum. Jennifer is a professional substitute teacher, a mother of three, a wife of one, and a storyteller living near the shores of Lake Michigan. Jennifer earned her Ductorate degree — the highest credential bestowed upon Disney University graduates — in the summer of 1993.

For you Disney history buffs, back then, Disney was fresh off a Best Picture Oscar nomination for Beauty and the Beast, Aladdin was red hot, and The Lion King was on the near horizon. As Jennifer remembers, "Disney was right at the forefront of innovating with CGI in animation." Jennifer brings us a first-hand look at the Disney curriculum, culture and experience directly from what she describes as "the epicenter" of innovation in entertainment, media and animated film production. If you're interested in applying for Disney's College Program, be sure to read about Jennifer's experiences. We believe they are quite illuminating.

Also, be aware that spots in this program are extremely limited, the application process is challenging, and the program is demanding. But if you do get it, you'll learn firsthand whether a job with Disney is right for you, and you'll get a leg up on the competition as you work to build a Disney career." ("What Is The Disney College Program?")

"The Disney College Program refers to an array of programs providing education, professional development, and paid internships through the Disney company. Founded in 1981, the educational sector of the Disney Company includes The Disney College Program for paid internships, the Disney University "cast member" training facilities, and a host of international programs included under the umbrella of the Walt Disney World International Exchange Program.

The program typically works alongside a traditional college degree program. Many traditional and online colleges have partnered with the Disney Company to give their students access to the Disney College Program. Roughly 5% of Disney employees have entered the company's workforce through the Disney College Program.

For a quick overview:

- The Disney College Program is a national internship program for U.S. residents, and includes locations at both the Walt Disney World Resort in Florida and the Disneyland Resort in California. This immersive experience — typically a semester in length — provides on-the-job training, housing, and college credits where eligible.
- The Disney University is the global training program for aspiring Disney "cast members" — employees who make up the expansive Disney team of performers, leaders, and skilled personnel. Most courses are administered on location at the Walt Disney World building adjacent to the Magic Kingdom in Orlando, Florida; Burbank's Team Disney Headquarters; and various learning facilities near both Disneyland Paris and Disneyland in Anaheim, California.
- The Walt Disney World International Exchange Program provides access to training programs and cast membership for international students through three distinct programs — the Academic Exchange Program; Cultural Representative Program; and the Cultural Exchange Program.

Though each of these experiences is distinguished by terms of eligibility and areas of focus, the Disney Company succeeds through a highly sophisticated measure of brand control, especially through its development of a well-defined employee culture. This begins with a thoughtfully constructed curriculum, immersive educational experiences, hands-on training, and focused professional development.

One feature that truly distinguishes a Disney education from a traditional campus experience is the compatibility between work and education. Disney University graduate Jennifer Tatum recalls:

The biggest difference between Disney dorms and university dorms is that work managers have the same goals as the school and educators do. Our education and our classes came first. Many of my friends in college struggled with a work/school balance because their employers weren't concerned about their education priorities or schedules. But that was never an issue in the Disney College program because everybody agreed we were there to learn, and work was always in support of that." ("What Is The Disney College Program?")

"The Walt Disney Co., which recently warned of slowing demand at its Experiences segment, is spending billions of dollars to expand its theme park attractions and its cruise ship fleet.

- Among the announcements the entertainment giant reported at its three-day "D23: The Ultimate Disney Fan Event" in Anaheim, Calif.: the largest expansion in the 53-year history of Orlando's Magic Kingdom.
- Disney announced a $60 billion, 10-year expansion of its theme parks and cruise operations last year.

The Walt Disney Co. (DIS), which recently warned of slowing demand at its Experiences segment, is spending billions of dollars to expand its theme park attractions and its cruise ship fleet.

The announcements by the entertainment giant over the weekend flesh out details of the $60 billion, 10-year expansion of its theme parks and cruise operations it announced last year.

Among the announcements the entertainment giant reported at its three-day "D23: The Ultimate Disney Fan Event" in Anaheim, Calif.: the largest expansion in the 53-year history of Orlando's Magic Kingdom, with a new Villains Land and another inspired by the "Cars" franchise; new

"Avengers" attractions in its California, Hong Kong, and Shanghai parks; and increasing its cruise ship fleet to 13 from nine by 2031.1

Experiences Segment Struggles With Consumer Pullback in Spending

Consumers' pullback on discretionary spending has affected Disney shares despite the company's better-than-expected third-quarter results last Wednesday, which saw its combined ESPN+, Disney+, and Hulu streaming unit turn a profit for the first time." (Gopalan) Disney is expanding their real estate, by creating more and more hotels, cruises etc. Recently Disney has launched a new cruise line called disney cruise, which has themed dining, character encounters, Broadway-style shows, and Castaway Cay, a private island, along with family-friendly activities and staterooms designed for comfort and magic.

"For the very first time, not only will we be projecting onto Sleeping Beauty's Castle, but also Main Street USA," said Tim Lutkin, artistic director of the production, referring to the park's main commercial artery lined with boutiques and merchandise.

The spectacle also reflects Disney's storytelling evolution. Lutkin noted the shift from classic ballgown tales to modern narratives like "Encanto" and "Inside Out 2," which delve into deeper themes such as anxiety and depression. The level of the latter's box office success, Lutkin said, "was a big surprise for everybody."

It was "an indicator the world and its relationship with Disney are ready to embrace more complex stories."

This shift is mirrored in the show's selection of movies, spanning Disney's timeless classics and emotionally resonant modern hits.

Disney Adventure World

At the heart of Disneyland Paris' expansion is the transformation of Walt Disney Studios Park, doubling in size and reimagined as Disney Adventure World. Opening in spring 2025, a new park entrance, World Premiere, will greet visitors with the glamour of a Hollywood film premiere, leading them into immersive themed areas.

"These projects reflect our commitment to innovation and storytelling," said Natacha Rafalski, head of Disneyland Paris, adding that they will further strengthen it as Europe's top tourist destination.

Already Europe's most-visited theme park and France's top tourist attraction outdrawing the Louvre, Disneyland Paris welcomed over 10 million visitors in 2023.

The expansion includes two eagerly awaited themed lands. The World of Frozen, debuting in 2026, will transport guests to Arendelle with a central lake hosting water performances and the Frozen Ever After boat ride, alongside themed dining, shopping, and accommodations. Meanwhile, The Lion King land will bring the Pride Lands to life with a long flume cascading from Pride Rock and encounters with beloved characters like Simba and Timon." (AP news)

"The Galactic Starcruiser faced a number of challenges during its limited run. Perhaps the greatest being the price and perceived value: The *New York Times* reported at the time Disney announced it would close that the starting cost was more than $4,800 for two people and around $6,000 for a family of four.

Before its new use was confirmed, fans speculated that the building could be made into a more digestible *Star Wars*-themed experience, such as a dinner show that would make use of the Halcyon ship's large dining room and other worldly menu or the moody bar-lounge off the lobby that could have potentially drawn visitors.

Transportation may have been a contributing factor in the decision to not have the building be accessible to guests going forward.

The "pods" that shuttled hotel guests to and from the nearby *Star Wars* Galaxy's Edge land could only hold a few people and entailed a bumpy, somewhat claustrophobic journey through backstage areas. The main entrance to the hotel's earthly launch pad was in an un-themed parking area disconnected from the park.

While office space sounds dull on the surface, the projects being worked on there are some of the most intriguing coming to Disney World in the next several years.

At the Disney Experiences showcase at D23 in August, it was revealed that a new *Indiana Jones*-themed ride and *Encanto*-themed ride will arrive at Disney's Animal Kingdom in 2027.

Billy Crystal appeared onstage at the convention to announce that a *Monsters Inc.* land will be coming to Disney's Hollywood Studios. There, a ride that travels through the door factory from the film will mark the first-ever suspended coaster for a Disney park." (Schmidt)

"At the Disney Experiences showcase at D23 on Saturday, Aug. 10, exciting changes coming to Walt Disney World in Orlando, Florida, were announced.

Josh D'Amaro, the Chairperson of Walt Disney Parks and Resorts, revealed that a new *Indiana Jones*-themed ride will arrive at Disney's Animal Kingdom, as Bruce Vaughn, the Chief Creative Officer of Walt Disney Imagineering, later joined him to discuss an *Encanto*-themed ride that will join the theme park's attractions. Both will debut in 2027.

Then, Billy Crystal appeared onstage to announce that a *Monsters Inc.* land will be coming to Disney's Hollywood Studios. There, a ride that travels through the door factory from the film will mark the first-ever suspended coaster for a Disney park." (Avila and Rice)

New and new things are getting added to disney, from Star Wars themed experience, to new cruise lines to make the imagination into reality.

STAR
WARS

Rights of Marvels and Starwars

Marvel is a common subsidiary to Disney and provides a lot of viewers.

"Marvel feels like it's in the worst spot. What used to be a must-see slate of films and hype-creating shows has become a slog, an attempt to recreate the magic that led up to Avengers Endgame, which they'll never be able to do.

Marvel has released some truly bad movies as of late, the most obvious one being Ant-Man and the Wasp: Quantumania, which was a very long introduction for Kang, the new supervillain who is very much Not Thanos and is very much in limbo with his actor facing assault charges and other accusations. But also what should have been surefire hits like Thor: Love and Thunder and Multiverse of Madness were not. The best Marvel movie in this recent era has been Guardians of the Galaxy Vol. 3, but now Marvel has lost James Gunn who has gone over to run DC, which is not great for them.

The television streaming era for Marvel has been absolutely all over the place in terms of the both the qualities of the shows, but also how they're handled heading into the future:

Loki – Probably the best, most cohesive, fun series Disney has had. Renewed for season 2 (about to air) relevant to the larger storyline without being absolutely necessary to see. Great job.

WandaVision – A good show by itself, but it shows the remaining disconnect between Marvel movies and Marvel TV, as where they took Wanda after this show into Multiverse of Madness made absolutely no sense.

The Falcon and the Winter Soldier – The definition of a show that did not need to exist. It's effectively a six episode explanation of Falcon getting his Captain America costume, but it could be cut and there would be nothing lost between Endgame and Captain America 4.

Hawkeye – A very good show with the charming Hailee Steinfeld as a great new hero, Kate Bishop. When will we see Kate Bishop again? No one has any idea. There's apparently no second season of this show nor any word we will ever see her in a movie. Bizarre.

She-Hulk – A deeply different experiment that attempted to channel the playfulness and goofiness of She-Hulk in the comics, but was lambasted by Very Angry Men who did not like its feminist messaging or comic-like asides like She-Hulk twerking (in the comics, She-Hulk famously jump-roped naked in one sequence). There seemed to be little room in the Marvel universe for a flat-out comedy, even if it did its job well and the meta ending was one of the most prescient things we've seen out of the universe. It did need additional help with its CGI, however, and of course, we have zero idea if it's getting a season 2 or if we'll ever see Jen, Bruce or Bruce's son again.

Ms. Marvel – Iman Vellani is the best-cast Marvel character since Tony Stark's Iron Man. But her show was not as good as she was in the role. Now, again, we probably have forgotten a season 2 for Velani to co-star in The Marvels, which is better than Kate Bishop got, but it's unclear what they will do with her after that.

Secret Invasion – One of the worst things Marvel has ever made, and the most money they've ever set on fire with a shocking $200 million budget. Deeply boring, pointless and a fraction of what a more interesting story was in the comics, it was the biggest miss of this entire era, possibly even including Quantumania." (Tassi)

Star Wars and Marvel are big subparts of Disney, there are many fans and different fanbases for the same.

"For many die-hard sci-fi fans, having to choose between the two feels like having to choose a favorite child. For others, the winner is obvious. I belong to the former group. Though *Star Wars* was the dawn of my sci-fi/cinematic infatuation, I later discovered the world of Marvel. Both series share many similarities, including plots that transcend planets and galaxies, with stories of many characters intertwined. *Star Wars* has undoubtedly left a brilliant legacy (though subseries are constantly emerging) while Marvel continues building its exalted narrative today.

Both series have had an immense impact on the global film industry, generating enormous fan bases and enormous profit. Initially, I wondered if the two could even be compared objectively. Regardless, I was determined to settle the long-standing debate. Here is a deep dive comparison between *Marvel Cinematic Universe* (MCU) and *Star Wars*.

Plot

The narratives of both the *Star Wars* saga and MCU are complex–involving many characters and always leaving more to be uncovered. While the *Star Wars* saga is a series of 12 movies that are part of one extended plot, MCU is composed of over 30 films. Most of the MCU movies are individual hero's stories that make up a larger narrative of the Avengers and the Universe as a whole. Both of these sci-fi/fantasy series depict epic conflicts and intergalactic battles of good vs. evil.

The characters in *Star Wars* are more compelling and flawed than the characters in Marvel, and therefore more realistic. Since the *Star Wars* saga has fewer films, the story revolves around fewer characters. As a result, the *Star Wars* films build a more complex background and story of development for each character. Viewers can relate on a deeper level to the stories of *Star Wars* characters whereas the superheroes of Marvel develop in a way that is entertaining, but not as raw and relatable.

The plot of *Star Wars* is also deep in the sense that many of its major conflicts are analogies to current-day world issues. For example, the recurring conflict in *Star Wars* is the power of the "dark side" and the Empire, a tyrannical government trying to dominate the Resistance or the "light side" of the Force. This is symbolic of the struggle some people face today in countries with corrupt governments.

<u>Setting</u>

As many of us know, *Star Wars* takes place *a long time ago, in a galaxy far, far away,* following characters from planet to planet, while Marvel mostly takes place on current-day planet Earth. Several Marvel films including *Guardians of the Galaxy, Thor, Captain Marvel, Avengers: Infinity War, and Avengers: Endgame* take MCU's narrative to new worlds and galaxies, establishing dynamic settings, not unlike Star Wars.

That said, Star Wars does it better. The artistry and creative brilliance that went into each planet in the Star Wars saga is apparent. From the nearly inhospitable, icy terrain of *Hoth* to the lush, evergreen forests of *Endor* to the barren deserts of *Tatooine* to the picturesque, Arcadian landscapes of *Naboo*, the planets of Star Wars have it all. Not only is the setting elevated by the invention of planets, but also by the imaginative nuance of each establishing shot, each deep space scene, each battleship sequence, and each starship chase. I can't think of another movie or series of films that continually makes me wish to transcend the screen into its universe like *Star Wars* does. Inflicting viewers with such a sense of longing is a feat of creative genius.

<u>**Cinematography**</u>

The first *Star Wars* film, *A New Hope* (Episode IV in the series), made its debut in 1977. Now four decades old, the original *Star Wars* trilogy is said to have paved the way for modern cinema and special effects. The first film created by MCU, *Iron Man*, debuted in 2008. Film quality undeniably improved between the release o*f A New Hope* and the release of *Iron Man*. Comparing the graphics, artistry, and animation between the two films, *Iron Man* beats *A New Hope* in visual appeal. However, it is important to consider the fact that the first *Star Wars* trilogy was extremely advanced for its time. The first *Star Wars* films "pioneered the use of computers in special effects filmmaking, and essentially invented the modern Hollywood special effects house," devoted film critic and *Star Wars* expert Peter Suderman said. MCU undoubtedly continues to produce some of the most visually stunning films in the industry. Needless to say, Marvel would never have been able to achieve the level of excellence it has today if *Star Wars* had not come before it. The three most recent *Star Wars* films display this same level of visual brilliance, with scenes that are true works of art." (Ervine)

"Both the MCU and *Star Wars* saga are impressive. The series share elements of stunning cinematography, intricate plots, a multitude of characters, enormous and diverse fanbases, and extensive profit. As *Star Wars* preceded Marvel, it paved the way for future sci-fi cinema and, therefore, Marvel could not exist without *Star Wars*. Marvel, being the more current of the two series, is the "*Star Wars*" of a new era. Yet, there is nothing quite like the nostalgia that so many feel when rewatching the earlier *Star Wars* films, as its story transcends the screen and is held in the hearts of an entire generation." (Ervine)

"Both the MCU and *Star Wars* franchises are independently owned by Disney and are the two highest-grossing cinematic franchises in the world. Marvel takes number one and *Star Wars* number two, which is mainly because MCU has produced dozens of films whereas *Star Wars* comprises just 12. Both series have generated enormous fan bases worldwide. Their popularity has given rise to theme parks, a multitude of video games and subseries, as well as billions of dollars worth of merchandise, all inspired by the films. As far as global popularity, *Star Wars* expectedly takes the lead. While the plot and characters of *Star Wars* pertain to more universal themes, "Marvel's superheroes are distinctly American icons," superhero fanatic and journalist, Tim Webber said. Though the characters in Marvel never claim to be particularly patriotic, apart from Captain America, they "are still informed by American ideals on a foundational level," Webber said. The creation of *Star Wars*, on the other hand, turned into a worldwide pop-culture phenomenon, bringing fans together around the globe. Sci-fi fanatics in other countries likely find the narrative of *Star Wars* more appealing and more relatable than that of MCU." (Ervine)

"It was to be expected to be fair; Disney has moved the Star Wars based comics to Marvel starting from next year, when the next film is released. Walt Disney purchased Lucasfilm in 2012 and many fans believed that Marvel will regain the rights to produce comic books based around the world of Star Wars immediately, seeing that Disney also owns Marvel. It will now happen in 2015, which will coincide with the release of Star Wars episode VIII. Marvel did a long run of Star Wars comics in the late 70's and 80's – telling the story of what happened in the saga in between the movies.
"Dark Horse Comics published exceptional Star Wars comics for over 20 years," said Carol Roeder, director of Lucasfilm franchise publishing, Disney Publishing Worldwide said in a press statement, "and we will always be grateful for their enormous contributions to the mythos, and the terrific partnership that we had.

In 2015, the cosmic adventures of Luke, Han, Leia and Chewbacca will make the lightspeed jump back to Marvel, to begin a new age of adventures within the Star Wars universe."

"We here at Marvel could not be more excited to continue the publication of Star Wars comic books and graphic novels," said Marvel Worldwide Publisher and President, Dan Buckley. "The perennial brand of Star Wars is one of the most iconic in entertainment history and we are honored to have the opportunity to bring our creative talent pool to continue, and expand Star Wars into galaxies far, far away.”

“We’re incredibly excited by this next chapter in the Star Wars saga,” said Andrew B. Sugerman, executive vice president of Disney Publishing Worldwide. “Bringing together the iconic Lucasfilm and Marvel brands to tell new stories will allow us to continue to thrill lovers of the original Star Wars comic books and entertain generations to come.” (Burgees)

Marvel has a lot of rights as well, given to 20th century fox and other companies as well.

"See in 1998, Marvel began licensing the rights to put some of its characters in films to other studios. Marvel first licensed the film rights to the character Blade to New Line Cinema. Soon after 20th Century Fox got the license for X-Men and then Sony got the film rights to Spider-Man.

By 2004, Marvel Studios realized they were only getting a fraction of the millions and billions these other studios were making off of their characters. So that Marvel Studios secured money to be able to produce its own films and get some of their characters back. So now we have three major studios all making different Marvel movies.

So it's understandable that fans and audiences would be a bit confused as to which characters are owned by which studios.

Now I've seen plenty of posts out there try to make sense of it and some of them do a decent job. This image from TheTwinGeeks.com isn't bad and is a nice general start :

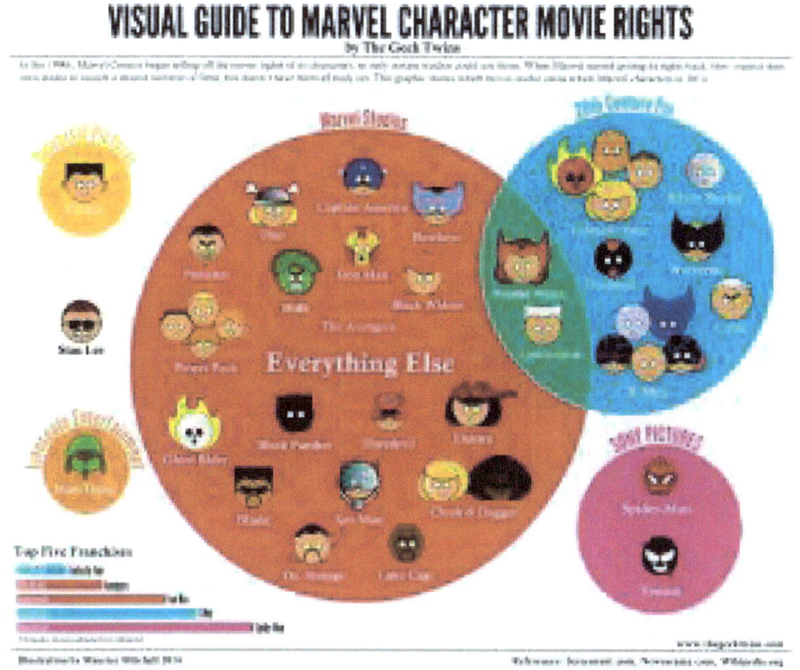

I tend to think 20th Century Fox should be a little bigger because while technically Marvel Studios owns more film rights, Fox owns the bigger and more recognizable names. I think it's also important to make note of past films and the history there.

For instance, Universal had the film rights to the Hulk and made the 2003 Ang Lee film. Marvel got the rights back and did *The Incredible Hulk* in 2008 as part of their Phase 1. A lot of people get it confused and think Marvel Studios did the 2003 film as well. It's confusing because *Incredible Hulk* was a soft reboot. They didn't do a Hulk origin story and it seems like a sequel to the 2003 movie but it's not connected.

Also we're now starting to get more TV Shows going and Marvel is connecting some of these to their cinematic universe so I believe they deserve a mention as well. In addition to movies, WB is doing a lot with their animated movies and TV shows.

My goal here is to try to get a more complete list of what we know so far and give a little background. I'm also going to do a Pro/Con list for each of the major studios because I think there are different strengths and weaknesses for each one depending on the film rights they own.

I'm going to try to keep this list updated as much as possible as things change. Don't expect to see many changes for the major characters though. Even when a film isn't good critically, most of these big name characters still rake in a ton of money. So don't expect rights to X-Men or Spider-Man to revert any time soon (or ever). Chances are, that will never happen." (mtrnetwork)

Now talking about the rights of Star Wars, "However, the transaction didn't immediately move over all Star Wars rights to Disney. While the Mouse House obviously owns everything post-merger (beginning with The Force Awakens), they still have to wait to get their hands on most of the pre-Disney catalog. Fox owns the rights to The Empire Strikes Back, Return of the Jedi, and the entire prequel trilogy until May 2020. Because they were partners with Lucas on the seminal 1977 original, they will own A New Hope in perpetuity, which would make it somewhat difficult for Disney to release the inevitable "complete Skywalker saga" Blu-ray collection after Episode IX comes out. Of course, there's a development making plenty of headlines that will change all that in the near future.

Disney, of course, is in the process of acquiring Fox's entertainment properties, after shareholders agreed to the groundbreaking merger. In the wake of this news, most of the discussion has been in regards to the integration of the X-Men and Fantastic Four into the Marvel Cinematic Universe, but the deal has ramifications for Star Wars as well. With Disney buying Fox, it means they'll secure those precious New Hope rights and own all of the Star Wars movies. This may not exactly be what people had in mind when they said Disney and Fox needed to come to an agreement to settle the New Hope rights, but it'll get the job done.

What this doesn't do, however, is change anything concerning the much-theorized (but never official) release of the unaltered original trilogy on Blu-ray. That is Lucasfilm's call to make, and there are no signs to indicate they're going to change their stance on that matter. The 2011 versions (and all the alterations that came with them) are considered official franchise canon, and Kathleen Kennedy is of the mind to leave Lucas' films alone while she concentrates on building Star Wars' future. Perhaps one day this will change, but for now audiences will have to make do with what's available. Disney would happily rake in the revenue such a box set would bring in, though they're certainly in good shape with the new movies they're releasing.

Star Wars Movie Television Rights

A lot of fans own their own copies of the movies in their Blu-ray collections, but television networks are keen on acquiring the broadcast rights for the popular franchise. In the case of the first six Star Wars movies, those are currently owned by Turner, meaning they can air on

TNT and TBS. The deal runs until 2024, which explains why Disney was looking to acquire the rights from Turner. However, it isn't going to be easy. Per the reports, Turner wants significant compensation, including money and programming. Discussions between the two parties haven't gone far, and it remains to be seen if anything becomes of this.

The post-merger Star Wars films were not part of Lucasfilm's deal with Turner, and instead are on Netflix as part of the Mouse House's arrangement with the streaming giant that went into effect beginning with 2016 theatrical releases. As of this writing, both Rogue One and The Last Jedi are available for viewing. Since all Disney-era Star Wars films are part of this, it stands reason to believe Solo will hit Netflix at some point, perhaps after it hits digital and Blu-ray this fall. However, this practice is coming to an end very soon." (Agar)

Food and Beverage

We have seen that Disney has hotels, cruises etc, but disney also offers food and beverages. For example at disneyland they have mickeymouse shaped pancakes, different types of churros and what not!

"With more dishes than ever to try, you're going to want to attend both nights of the Food & Wine Classic. And it's important to note that the menus for each food station are different on Friday versus Saturday.
"The culinary experience is a key element of that [Disney] magic. We showcase our innovation in food and beverage with constantly evolving offerings which give us an opportunity to present new flavors, styles, and approaches," explains Sherman. "We empower our culinary team to bring forth ideas and concepts that are certain to surprise and delight our guests."

On Friday, guests can try some of the innovations in food such as hand-crafted smoked bacon with braised greens, carrot purée, artisanal bread purée, and shaved vinegar heirloom apple from Smokin' D's BBQ. Another highlight of the Friday menu is a new dish of hand-made harissa spiced lamb sausage that's served alongside bulgar wheat, smoked yogurt, and fennel onion salad.

Saturday brings an all-new menu to try at some stands. From The Fountain, you can try a Reuben sandwich with pickled mustard seed, Russian dressing, house-cured cabbage, and marble rye bread. An all-new dish to the festival lineup for Saturday is the Korean "No Mayo" Salad, with rice noodles, bean sprouts, cucumber, kimchi, and cashews.

Some of the more popular restaurants at the resort complex will host the same menu on both nights of the festival. This is the case for Shula's Steak House, where Roasted Linz Heritage Black Angus Beef Tenderloin served with marble potatoes, caramelized onion purée, horseradish, and béarnaise sauce will be served on Friday and Saturday. Todd English's Bluezoo will also feature the same menu of Roasted Sablefish with black garlic miso butter and a Shaved Asparagus Salad with cured yellowfin tuna as its two dishes. Rosa Mexicano rounds out the restaurants serving the same menu. At this booth, there will be tempura-fried cauliflower tacos, fish tacos, and the restaurant's signature guacamole.

Food & Wine Classic will have four themed food areas that will serve the same menu on Friday and Saturday. The first is an ode to fresh Florida dishes at For The Love of Florida. Here, you'll find dishes like Seminole Pumpkin Fry Bread and Grilled Florida Oysters with a side of house-made kumquat hot sauce. At the Beer Garden, hot buffalo wings are always a hit — along with boiled peanuts and miso butter-tossed Brussels sprouts. Adults will instantly be brought back to childhood at Carnival Corner, where corn dog bites and chipotle macaroni and cheese are on the menu. An all-new dessert zone, called Pastry, will feature sweet delights like Caramel Banana Creme Brûlée, Mandarin Cream Beignets, and Chocolate Blackberry Choux Puff." (duBois)

The best disney world restaurants are below-

" **Worth It Splurge: Cinderella's Royal Table**

Location. Location. Location. Cinderella's Royal Table is probably the most hyped Disney World restaurant and it's worth the praise. The exclusive spot located inside Cinderella Castle has the most unique views of Magic Kingdom. And, yes, you get to meet a bunch of royals and there's a little autographed postcard from Cinderella. However, the real premium is the exclusive access inside a landmark that most only ever see from the outside. And the theming is incredible. What's more surprising: For a kid-first experience, the food is *good*. The prix fixe includes an app, entree, and dessert with choices ranging from filet mignon to a catch of the day with gouda grits. But whatever you do, don't sleep on The Clock Strikes Twelve tart. It comes with the most beautiful chocolate clock face. There are so many little details to Cinderella's Royal Table and while there are several spots around the resort with fine dining over $75 (or $100 if you add one of the various champagne flights), this is an experience that feels worth the cost.

Best Mobile Order: Casey's Corner

Walt Disney World Resort

On the corner of Main Street, U.S.A., most people cruise right past Casey's on the way to Cinderella Castle thinking it's just hot dogs. But there's something else on the menu that's more in-the-know among theme park regulars. Corn dog nuggets. That's right. Corn. Dog. Nuggets. And here's the semi-secret menu trick: You can buy hot pretzel cheese sauce to dip them in. For plant-based offerings at Disney World, you can't go wrong with a "sausage" dog in a potato bun. And right now, there's a frozen non-alcoholic mint julep lemonade that's giving us all the Tiana's Bayou Adventure vibes.

Best Reservation: Liberty Tree Tavern

Walt Disney World Resort

You know that full-as-a-tick bliss that happens at the end of a big Thanksgiving dinner? Imagine that feeling but you don't have to cook a thing. And it's available every day. Heaven is a place on Earth and it's Liberty Tree Tavern in Liberty Square. The family-style feast includes turkey, pot roast, mashed potatoes, mac 'n' cheese, stuffing (It's colonial theming so we'll forgive Mickey for not having cornbread dressing.), and more. But the real reason fans love LTT is the Oooey Gooey Toffee Cake. And because it's "all-you-care-to-enjoy," it's bottomless, never-ending Ooey Gooey Toffee Cake. Now, reservations are hard to come by because everyone wants that cake. Here's a pro tip: If you can't get a reservation for LTT, try The Diamond Horseshoe over in Frontierland. They now serve the exact same items. It's just called a Saloon Feast. And, yes, you can also get the cake there, too.

Best Lounge: Jungle Navigation Co. LTD Skipper Canteen

Technically, we're making a square with a circle here. Because, historically, Magic Kingdom is a dry park and that goes back to Walt Disney's original wishes for Disneyland and Disney World. However, Disney Parks have evolved and you can find spirits in bars, kiosks, carts, and more at Disney World's other parks. But at Magic Kingdom, alcohol is only available inside sit-down restaurants. So, if you're in need of ice-cold beer to cut through that Central Florida heat, plan ahead or take your chances with walk-ups at Jungle Navigation Co. LTD Skipper Canteen in Adventureland. The highly themed space inspired by the Jungle Cruise attraction features housemade sangrias, the Kungaloosh Spiced Excursion Ale made exclusively for Disney World, and a great margarita.

Best Mobile Order: Regal Eagle Smokehouse

Walt Disney World Resort

The American Pavilion at World Showcase doesn't have the biggest razzle dazzle attractions or rides, but they do have a tour of BBQ at Regal Eagle Smokehouse: Craft Drafts & Barbecue. All the great signature styles are there, from Memphis to Kansas City to North Carolina to Texas. (But we would love to petition for some Alabama sauce.) Fixin's include baked beans "with burnt ends," creamy coleslaw, and more. This writer does not agree with the direction they went in for the mac 'n' cheese. If you call a mac 'n' cheese baked, it should be a casserole with a thick cheesy crust. Not a basket of creamy noodles with a sprinkle of bread crumbs. However, the banana pudding is the epitome of Southern summer. And the near 50-50 pudding to wafer ratio is perfection. If you've got a hungry group, order one of everything, grab a picnic table outside and have a mini 'cue crawl.

Best Reservation: Tusker House Restaurant

Character dining at Disney World is a whole world of its own. But in reality, what you pay for is access to many characters within a short amount of time with no waiting in line. But breakfast at Tusker House is 10/10. This writer would pay for that buffet even if Mickey and friends weren't hanging around. Although, their little safari outfits are so stinking cute. Here, you'll find Nala and Simba waffles, mealie pap, which is like a cheesy cornbread-grits hybrid, and POG mimosas. POG juice is actually bottomless all day. Yes, infinite POG. Lunch and dinner have naan and breads with various dips and curries as well as Red Red, which is a side dish made from black-eyed peas and plantains. There are also honey plantains, but for the real sweets, you have to try the blueberry and banana pudding.

Best Lounge: Nomad Lounge

Walt Disney World Resort

Nomad Lounge is often mentioned as a silver lining alternative if you can't get a reservation at Tiffins because it's right next door and serves the beloved Tiffins bread service as well as similar fare for small bites. But Nomad Lounge is no second fiddle. It's a clutch oasis for escaping the heat in Animal Kingdom, which always seems 10 degrees hotter than any other park. This is porch sitting at its best as the lounge overlooks Discovery River and a wall of lush greenery that creates a serene vibe within the chaos and crowds. And the small bites are tasty, from pineapple-glazed pork belly to Impossible sliders that will impress any meat-loving grill pro. Try one of the many specialty cocktails or mocktails as Nomad Lounge has a large list of fun, creative zero-proof sips such as the Happy Macaque with guava and coffee syrup. For beer, don't miss the Kungaloosh Spiced Excursion Ale on draft. It's exclusive to Disney World and is brewed with sorghum.

Worth It Splurge: Tiffins Restaurant

Walt Disney World Resort

Now, to Tiffins. Fine dining in a theme park does exist and you'll find an exceptional meal at Tiffins Restaurant. Inspired by travels to Asia and Africa and research Disney Imagineers compiled while creating Animal Kingdom, the menu at Tiffins is like a traveler's notebook, from Szechuan noodles to Oaxacan pork. And the shrimp and grits with South African mealie pap will have you rethinking everything you know about this classic dish. There's even a salad with lettuce straight from The Land's garden at EPCOT. But you cannot eat at Tiffins without starting with the signature bread service which includes guava sauce and a ginger-pear chutney. Some things at Disney are overhyped. These dips and condiments are worthy." (Revel)

"While Disney has long used food design as a way of elevating its traditional fare, it entered a new phase of innovation in 2017 when it launched its theme park land based on the planet Pandora from James Cameron's film "Avatar."

With this new land, Disney had the opportunity to create its own cuisine. It wasn't translating foreign dishes and recreating them at Epcot, it was taking inspiration from a film about an alien planet. Chefs used spices found in Argentinian, Brazilian and Chinese cooking to bring a distinct flavor profile to its food. "It expands the experience," said Bill Coan, president and CEO of iTEC Entertainment.

"Disney is playing this out and playing it up to advance the visitor experience and at the same time generate incremental revenue."

Guests tend to be less stringent about their diets while on vacation and will opt to try out menu items that they cannot get anywhere else, Coan said.

At Satu'li Canteen, guests make their own grain bowls, choosing between a base of quinoa and vegetable salad, red and sweet potato hash, mixed whole grain and rice or romaine and kale salad.

Then they add either grilled chicken, roasted beef, shrimp or chili-spiced tofu on top as well as a variety of dressing options. Each has been designed to have an out-of-this-world look that is both appetizing and photographable.

Instagram has become a place for parkgoers to share their food experience at the parks with others and to get ideas of what they should try in the future.

Pandora also has an array of alcoholic and nonalcoholic drinks available from Pongu Pongu, a themed Tiki bar located near the canteen." (Whitten)

Disney does has some yum food and in the most interesting shapes as well, which resemble their disney characters.

Reference List

Adamson, Thomas. "Disneyland Paris touts spectacular nighttime show using Paris Games laser technology." 19 Jan 2025, https://apnews.com/article/france-disneyland-lasers-693295b13a3982986594ecf86f3b21c7. Accessed 14 March 2025.

Agar, Chris. "Star Wars Rights Explained: What Disney Does (And Doesn't) Own." 10 Aug 2018, https://screenrant.com/star-wars-movie-tv-rights-explained/. Accessed 18 March 2025.

Aithor. "Disney's Streaming Service Integration." Aithor, 10 Feb 2025, https://aithor.co.in/essay-examples/disneys-streaming-service-integration. Accessed 7 Mar 2025.

AllEars. "Why Disney has to keep solving." 19 May 2019, https://allears.net/2019/05/19/why-disney-has-to-keep-changing/. Accessed 7 March 2025.

AP news. "Disneyland Paris touts spectacular nighttime show using Paris Games laser technologyDisneyland Paris touts spectacular nighttime show using Paris Games laser technology." 19 Jan 2025, https://apnews.com/article/france-disneyland-lasers-693295b13a3982986594ecf86f3b21c7. Accessed 18 March 2025.

Avila, Daniela, and Nicholas Rice. "Disney Announces a Villains Land, Monsters Inc. Land, Encanto Ride Plus More Coming to Walt Disney World." People, 12 Aug 2024, https://people.com/disney-announces-a-monsters-inc-land-new-rides-at-walt-disney-world-8693558. Accessed 18 Mar 2025.

Burgees, Carl. "Marvel handed rights to produce Star Wars comics." screencitirx, 3 Jan 2014, https://screencritix.com/marvel-handed-rights-to-produce-star-wars-comics/. Accessed 18 March 2025.

business wire. "The Walt Disney company." Accessed 21 Dec 24.

celinayebba. "The Walt Disney Company." *disney corp research paper - Hospitality Research Paper*, coursehero, 4th July 2008, https://www.coursehero.com/file/79607/disney-corp-research-paper/. Accessed 7 March 2025.

"Detailed PESTEL Analysis of Disney." *EdrawMax*, https://www.edrawmax.com/article/disney-pestel-analysis.html. Accessed 16 November 2024.

disney. "disney swot analysis." disney, https://businessmodelanalyst.com/disney-swot-analysis/?utm_campaign={{campaign.name}}&utm_source=google-ads&utm_medium=cpc&utm_content={{ad.name}}&utm_term={{adset.name}}&ad_id={{ad.id}}&gad_source=1&gclid=CjoKCQiAouG5BhDBARIsAOco8RT7-4kee_XbIQHTD1fRd2vbue. Accessed 16 nov 2024.

disney. "How Disney Became The World's Entertainment Leader." https://www.cascade.app/studies/disney-strategy-study#The-Brand-of-Disney. Accessed 3 jan 2025.

disney. "Mastering the Magic: An In-Depth Analysis of Disney's Organizational Structure." Accessed 21 dec 24.

Disney. "Winning in the OTT Era with Disney+ Hotstar." Accessed 21 dec 2024.

"Disney Channel Celebrates 40 Years of Imaginative, Iconic Programming." *The Walt Disney Company*, 18 April 2023, https://thewaltdisneycompany.com/disney-channel-celebrates-40-years-of-imaginative-iconic-programming/. Accessed 21 December 2024.

"Disney History." *D23*, https://d23.com/disney-history/. Accessed 11 October 2024.

"Disney History." *D23*, https://d23.com/disney-history/. Accessed 2 January 2025.

"Disney updates content warning for racism in classic films." *BBC*, 15 October 2020, https://www.bbc.com/news/world-us-canada-54566087. Accessed 7 March 2025.

Dorsey, Christopher. "History — Thank You Walt Disney." *Thank You Walt Disney*, https://www.thankyouwaltdisney.org/history. Accessed 4 November 2024.

duBois, Megan. "This Secret All-Inclusive Disney World Food Festival Features 45 Dishes and More Than 170 Beverages." 19 Sep 2024, https://www.foodandwine.com/walt-disney-world-swan-and-dolphin-food-and-wine-classic-8714433. Accessed 18 March 2025.

Dunn, Riley, and Charlie Hickman. "Should Disney keep making sequels?" *The Daily Iown*, daily iown, 18 June 2024, https://dailyiowan.com/2024/06/18/should-disney-keep-making-sequels/. Accessed 7 March 2025.

Ervine, Eleanor. "Marvel vs. Star Wars: An Intergalactic Debate." *https://thewestottawan.com/12316/opinion/marvel-vs-star-wars-an-intergalactic-debate/*, 14 March 2023, https://thewestottawan.com/12316/opinion/marvel-vs-star-wars-an-intergalactic-debate/. Accessed 18 March 2025.

everythingdiz. *SPONSORED Ultimate List Of The Highest Grossing Disney Movies Of All Time*. https://www.imdb.com/list/ls084411179/. Accessed 3 jan 2025.

Forbes. "How Disney Sailed Off With $1.6 Billion From Its Cruise Line." Accessed 21 dec 24.

Francis, Abey. "Case Study on Entrepreneurship: Walt Disney." *MBA Knowledge Base*, https://www.mbaknol.com/management-concepts/case-study-on-entrepreneurship-walt-disney/. Accessed 4 November 2024.

Goel, Yashika. "6 Heartwarming Disney Films on OTT for a Perfect Binge-Watching Session." TelecomTalk, 21 Aug 2023, https://telecomtalk.info/disney-films-on-ott-perfect-binge-watching/858858/. Accessed 7 March 2025.

Gopalan, Nisha. "Disney Announces Massive Theme Parks, Cruise Expansion at D23."

Investopedia, 12 Aug 2024, https://www.investopedia.com/disney-announces-massive-

theme-parks-cruise-expansion-at-d23-8693791?utm_source=chatgpt.com. Accessed 18

March 2025.

Harrisson, Juliette. "The Evolution of Disney Animation Over 100 Years of Art." *Den of*

Geek, 23 November 2023, https://www.denofgeek.com/movies/the-evolution-of-

disney-animation-over-100-years-of-art/. Accessed 6 March 2025.

Hart, Madison. "Disney's lack of diversity and use of racial stereotypes... a tale as old as

time." *King Street Chronicle*, 28 April 2022,

https://shgreenwichkingstreetchronicle.org/115987/opinions/disneys-lack-of-diversity-

and-use-of-racial-stereotypes-a-tale-as-old-as-time/. Accessed 7 March 2025.

mtrnetwork. "Marvel Character Movie Rights and Upcoming Movies."

https://www.mtrnetwork.net/marvel-character-movie-rights-upcoming-movies/.

Accessed 18 March 2025.

Rawson, Carissa, and Sally French. "What's the Difference Between Disneyland,

World?" *NerdWallet*, 21 July 2023, https://www.nerdwallet.com/article/travel/disney-

world-vs-disneyland-which-theme-park-should-you-choose. Accessed 11 December

2024.

Revel, Deanne. "The 24 Best Restaurants At Walt Disney World To Make Your Trip

Even More Magical." Sourthern Living, 14 Aug 2024,

https://www.southernliving.com/best-disney-world-restaurants-8694284. Accessed 18

March 2025.

Schmidt, Mackenzie. "Disney's Shuttered Star Wars Hotel Will Officially Be Converted

for a Much Less Magical Use After Over a Year." 4 Feb 2025,

https://people.com/disney-s-shuttered-star-wars-hotel-will-officially-be-converted-for-a-much-less-magical-use-8785706?utm_source=chatgpt.com. Accessed 18 Mar 2025. *Snow White becomes highest.*

Tassi, Paul. "Is Star Wars Or Marvel In Worse Shape Under Disney Right Now?" Forbes, 7 Sep 2023, https://www.forbes.com/sites/paultassi/2023/09/07/is-star-wars-or-marvel-in-worse-shape-under-disney-right-now/. Accessed 18 March 2025.

"What Is The Disney College Program?" *TheBestSchools.org*, 8 October 2024, https://thebestschools.org/magazine/disney-college-program/. Accessed 7 March 2025.

Whitten, Sarah. "From Dole Whip to Blue Milk: How Disney has used food to elevate its theme parks." CNBC, 6 Mar 2022, https://www.cnbc.com/2022/03/06/how-disney-has-used-food-to-elevate-its-theme-parks.html. Accessed 18 March 2025.